HARDY: THE MARGIN OF THE UNEXPRESSED

WRITING ON WRITING

Forthcoming titles in this series

Literature and Addiction
edited by Sue Vice, Matthew Campbell and Timothy Armstrong

Shakespeare and the New Europe
edited by Michael Hattaway, Boika Sokolova and Derek Roper

The Lover, the Dreamer and the World:
The Poetry of Peter Redgrove
by Neil Roberts

HARDY
The Margin
of the Unexpressed

Roger Ebbatson

Sheffield Academic Press

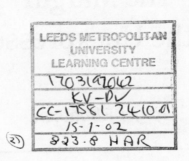
Copyright © 1993 Sheffield Academic Press

Published by Sheffield Academic Press Ltd
343 Fulwood Road
Sheffield S10 3BP
England

Typeset by Sheffield Academic Press
and
Printed on acid-free paper in Great Britain
by Biddles Ltd
Guildford

British Library Cataloguing in Publication Data

Ebbatson, Roger
Hardy: Margin of the Unexpressed
(Writing on Writing Series, ISSN 0966-7423)
I. Title II. Series
823.8

ISBN 1-85075-373-3
ISBN 1-85075-713-5 pa

CONTENTS

Preface   7
Acknowledgments   10
Key to Hardy Texts Cited   10

PART I
READING DESIRE

Chapter 1
Desperate Remedies (1871)   13

Chapter 2
The Trumpet-Major (1880)   43

Chapter 3
Our Exploits at West Poley (1883)   61

Chapter 4
Three Short Stories   73
    'On the Western Circuit' (1891)   73
    'An Imaginative Woman' (1893)   85
    'Barbara of the House of Grebe' (1890–91) 92

PART II
SPEAKING CLASS

Chapter 5
An Indiscretion in the Life of an Heiress (1878)   111

Chapter 6
'The Dorsetshire Labourer' (1883)   129

Bibliography   154
Index   158

PREFACE

My aims in this study are twofold: first, to explore some of the writings of Thomas Hardy from the varied perspectives of recent literary theory; secondly, to focus upon, and thus aid in the recuperation of, a selection of Hardy's 'minor' texts, works which have been systematically marginalized by critical and educational conformity. In order to work towards some dislocation of the liberal-idealist tradition which has successfully reproduced Hardy as a kind of cultural monument, I have abandoned chronology, preferring to pursue my analysis from within two differing but complementary perspectives. The work of the literary critic, Roland Barthes has suggested, consists of '*manhandling* the text, *interrupting* it',[1] and I have not hesitated to follow this prescription in allowing post-structuralist theory to percolate through the chosen texts. My title derives from Virginia Woolf's essay on Hardy. Woolf gives a superb definition of the experience of reading Hardy, suggesting that 'it is as if Hardy himself were not quite aware of what he did, as if his consciousness held more than he could produce'. It is this surplus of undecidability, this willingness of writer or reader to rest in uncertainty, which she memorably designates the 'margin of the unexpressed'.[2] I have attempted here, with an inevitable degree of failure, to eschew the compulsive critical drive towards interpretive mastery. It is Hardy's symptomatic ability to inscribe and express this inexpressible supplement or penumbra both in terms of movements of human desire through erotic exchange and of the interaction of classes in the countryside. The splitting and contradiction which his writing everywhere records, masks and voices specific, precariously maintained class and gender positions which vary from work to work, and sometimes from page to page. The work of literature, Pierre Macherey has argued, 'has its *margins*, an area of incompleteness from which we can observe its birth and its production',[3] and such observation is the project of the present study.

In dividing the book into two parts, I am seeking to alert the reader to a trajectory of reading which moves from a generally deconstruc-

tive perspective to a more wholly materialist approach. It has seemed
to me that some of the texts respond most fruitfully to a fundamentally dehistoricized, Lacanian–Derridean reading which relates textual
structure and language to questions of desire and the play of unconscious forces. Thus, the sensationalist *Desperate Remedies* and the
purportedly historicist *The Trumpet-Major* are subjected to readings
which begin, as it were, with Lacan; Hardy's children's story, *Our
Exploits at West Poley*, is explored in relation to Kristevan linguistics;
and selected short stories are exposed to a variety of post-structuralist
modes of inquiry. These are not, of course, the only approaches which
are feasible, but I hope the reader will find them, at the least, sugges-
tive. I am aware of the temptation to 'produce' texts which provide
the reader with a steady-state world from which the movement of
history has been expelled—indeed, this has been the overwhelming
end-product of the Hardy industry. But in relation to the texts
discussed in Part I, I would cite Macherey's contention that it is 'the
unconscious which is history', the play of history beyond the 'edges'
of the literary work, 'encroaching on those edges'.[4] Part II attempts a
more fully historicized reading of two Hardy texts, and it is my intention that the final emphasis of the book should be placed here.
Recourse to a literary-materialist context for *An Indiscretion in the
Life of an Heiress*, and to Bakhtin's sociolinguistics in the reading of
the Dorset labourer essay seeks to move beyond a deconstructive
technique which, in the hands of some of its practitioners, has theo-
rized away its own historicity and materiality in language. In wishing
to contribute to the current debate about Hardy, I come down finally
on the side of those critics whose readings foreground the historical
materialism of his texts. If the first part of my study seeks to unfix the
ground beneath the human subject, then the second part attempts to
return the subject, the text and the author to history. Some words of
Rosa Luxembourg's seem to me pertinent to our contemporary
understanding of Hardy: 'The logic of the historic process', she
writes, 'comes before the logic of the human beings who participate in
the historic process'.[5] It is the contention of this study that the literary
work is essentially a sublimation of the kinds of conflict which inhabit
language itself, and that it is these sites of conflict which endow the
Hardy texts with their enduring and provocative interest for us.

Notes

1. R. Barthes, *S/Z* (trans. R. Miller; London: Cape, 1975), p. 15.
2. Virginia Woolf, *Collected Essays* (London: Hogarth Press, 1968), p. 258.
3. P. Macherey, *A Theory of Literary Production* (trans. G. Wall; London: Routledge & Kegan Paul, 1978), p. 90.
4. Macherey, *Literary Production*, p. 94.
5. Cited in M. Ryan, *Marxism and Deconstruction* (Baltimore: Johns Hopkins University Press, 1982), p. 115.

ACKNOWLEDGMENTS

The chapter on *The Trumpet-Major* was first published in an earlier version as the introduction to the Penguin Classics edition of the novel. I am grateful to the staff of the Peirson Library, Worcester College of Higher Education, for their assistance in obtaining books; to Catherine Neale for her advice and encouragement; and to Lisa Needham for her expert typing.

KEY TO HARDY TEXTS CITED

ILH   *An Indiscretion in the Life of an Heiress* (ed. T. Coleman; London: Hutchinson, 1985).

CP   *The Complete Poems of Thomas Hardy* (ed. J. Gibson; London: Macmillan, 1978).

DP   *The Distracted Preacher and Other Tales* (ed. S. Hill; Harmondsworth: Penguin Books, 1979).

DR   *Desperate Remedies* (ed. P.N. Furbank; London: Macmillan, 1975).

OE   *Our Exploits at West Poley* (Oxford: Oxford University Press, 1981).

PW   *Thomas Hardy's Personal Writings* (ed. H. Orel; London: Macmillan, 1976).

TM   *The Trumpet-Major* (ed. R. Ebbatson; Harmondsworth: Penguin Books, 1987).

PART I

READING DESIRE

Chapter 1

DESPERATE REMEDIES (1871)

In the founding moment of *Desperate Remedies*, Hardy's imagination works with all the boldness of a beginning author—an author beginning his career and his story. Cytherea Graye sits in Hocbridge Town Hall awaiting a public reading from Shakespeare. One of the windows frames the 'upper part of a neighbouring church spire, now in course of completion under the superintendence of Miss Graye's father, the architect to the work' (*DR*, p. 45). The image takes on the uncanny significance of a dream:

> The picture thus presented to a spectator in the Town Hall was curious and striking. It was an illuminated miniature, framed in by the dark margin of the window, the keen-edged shadiness of which emphasised by contrast the softness of the objects enclosed (*DR*, p. 46).

The men on the spire are separated 'from the sphere and experiences of ordinary human beings' (*DR*, p. 46). Suddenly Cytherea's father 'indecisively laid hold of one of the scaffold-poles':

> In stepping, his foot slipped. An instant of doubling forward and sideways, and he reeled off into the air immediately disappearing downwards (*DR*, pp. 46-47).

As John Bayley wittily remarks, 'Mr Graye could easily, it appears, have vanished *upwards*'.[1] This seminal scene, with its anticipations of *The Master Builder*, may be glossed by means of Paul de Man's account of the 'creative leap', as an announcement of Hardy's predicament as a writer.

The work of art, de Man argues, 'must become a project aimed toward an unreachable goal' and its partial success takes on the form of 'a renunciation at the very moment when it comes into being'.[2] In the inaugurating paternal fall Hardy simultaneously lays claim to his artistic territory and seeks self-obliteration in a movement which enables his heroine to enter 'that labyrinth into which she stepped immediately afterwards' (*DR*, p. 45). Prior to this moment Cytherea has stood 'upon the extreme posterior edge of a tract in her life, in which the real meaning of Taking Thought had never been known' (*DR*, p. 45). De Man seeks to erase the distinction between author and reader, claiming that both engage 'in the same perilous enterprise': 'The artist projects himself into the future of his work as if it were possible to maintain an authentic temporality, but at the same time he knows this to be impossible'. In *Desperate Remedies*, that is, Hardy 'acts like an adventurer in entering upon a domain that he knows to lie beyond his reach'.[3] The writer exists within two different experiences of time: the temporality of quotidian existence and the time of the artist 'carried aloft', like Mr Graye, 'in the ambiguous time-structure of the monadic work'. De Man's argument takes the form of a commentary upon some ideas about the 'suspended' state of the artistic consciousness in Ludwig Binswanger, a philosopher who 'understands the urge to leap out of historical and everyday time'.[4] Trapped within the contingent world, the first reaction of the artist will be what Binswanger calls the 'march into the distance', a search for new experience which is undertaken 'without having to leave the horizontal expanse of the world'.[5] De Man argues that because artistic confinement is due 'not only to a lack of space, but is primarily caused by the excessive presence of time, these movements of horizontal expansion can never free the artist from his initial predicament'.[6] This contention is borne out by Cytherea's experience later, when she is subjected to the importunities of Aeneas Manston on the Knapwater Estate:

> The stillness oppressed and reduced her to mere passivity. The only wish the humidity of the place left in her was to stand motionless. The helpless flatness of the landscape gave her, as it gives all such temperaments, a sense of bare equality with, and no superiority to, a single entity under the sky (*DR*, p. 252).

The selfhood of the artist, and the concomitant 'fragility of poetic transcendence', is represented to the imagination by 'the anxieties associated with the feelings of height', feelings which may translate themselves, de Man believes, into dreams of 'involuntary ascent' and the 'upward fall'.[7] If the act of creation is akin to such acts of levitation, it seems inevitably accompanied by a 'possibility of falling and of dependency that follows such moments of flight', just as the somnambulistically powerful effects of the first half of *Desperate Remedies* dwindle into the detective machinations of the second half. The artist may ascend 'above the limits of his own self' into a state of false consciousness:[8] these limits may be discerned in the very structure of *Desperate Remedies*. If, as de Man argues, 'the kind of knowledge contained in art is specifically the knowledge of this fall',[9] then Mr Graye's descent should be read as a symptom of the writer's predicament. Through the exercise of literary rhetoric the writer, de Man posits, 'radically suspends logic and opens up vertiginous possibilities of referential aberration'.[10] Mr Graye's is the 'fortunate fall' which, by separating the heroine from home and herself, creates a narrative in the gap thereby opened up. Textuality is born out of the plunge into separation. Representation, as Jacques Derrida remarks, '*in the abyss of presence is not an accident of presence*'. On the contrary, the desire for presence is 'born from the abyss (the indefinite multiplication) of representation'.[11] Death of the father, then, plunges Cytherea into the abyss of representation: at that moment she enters the 'labyrinth' of the symbolic order via the plot devised for her by 'the architect to the work', Thomas Hardy.

The trajectory of the body falling through the air also serves as a potent emblem of what Harold Bloom, following the exposition of Epicurean philosophy in Lucretius, designates *clinamen*, the way a writer 'swerves away from his precursor'.[12] Creative activity begins, Bloom asserts, with an awareness that '*we are falling*'.[13] The poet, under this account, faces two choices: to accept the deity of cultural history, 'the embarrassments of a tradition grown too wealthy to need anything more', or to extinguish the 'talented poet who never quite made it'.[14] Hardy's avowed project in *Desperate Remedies* is, at the behest of George Meredith, to cannibalize the sensation novels of Ainsworth, Braddon and Collins; subconsciously, the work seeks to feed upon and destroy more potent precursors such as Shelley and George Eliot, and to escape the troubling oppressiveness of that supreme literary father whose work is being recited in the town hall. These contradictions make up the textual polyphony of *Desperate Remedies*, a novel which functions through deliberate misprision of a fictional tradition by means of Hardy's 'creative swerve'. The *clinamen*, Bloom urges, 'always must be considered as though it were simultaneously intentional and involuntary, the Spiritual Form of each poet *and* the gratuitous gesture each poet makes as his falling body hits the floor of the abyss'.[15] The work of fiction, as Pierre Macherey explains, 'begins to swerve from the enabling model which it had adopted', and thus begins to speak 'with several voices at once'.[16]

Paradoxically, the moment of awakening into representation and self-division is, for Cytherea, the first of two fainting fits which serve as frames to the narrative, and which repeat the collapse of Cytherea Aldclyffe in the story's prehistory. Cytherea is characterized by the reifying effect of the narrator's comments about her 'flexibility and elasticity' (*DR*, p. 44); the intense struggle to find her own voice issues in a 'convulsive movement' in which she 'could utter no sound' (*DR*, p. 47). On awakening she observes the effects of light from within a dreamlike state which will mark her future progress. The 'white sunlight shining in shaft-like lines from a rift in a slaty cloud' (*DR*, p. 47) becomes emblematic of the scene from the town hall windows. This ambiguous image expresses, overtly, feelings of filial regret; covertly, perhaps, a type of parricidal wish-fulfilment and emergence into sexual adulthood. In the course of his analysis of the dream-work, Freud concluded that dreams of falling were 'characterised by anxiety', and went on:

> Their interpretation offers no difficulty in the case of women, who almost always accept the symbolic use of falling as a way of describing a surrender to an erotic temptation.[17]

Looking back on the novel in 1889, Hardy expressed a wish to preserve in 'fragmentary form' only certain striking scenes.[18] This may have been authorial pose, but it signals a marked characteristic of inorganic dispersal which is highly developed in this text. The characters rarely fit the melodrama of the events: the 'worthy' characters— Springrove, Owen Graye, Cytherea herself—remain as inscrutable to themselves as do the more sensational personalities of Miss Aldclyffe or Aeneas Manston. These are subjects in whom may be observed what Roland Barthes designated 'a dispersion of energy in which there remains neither a central core nor a structure of meaning'.[19] The plot mechanism labours to produce unity, but Hardy's delight in the seductions of writing results in continuous Barthesian dispersion. Indeed, the 'perpetual production' of the writing celebrated by Barthes leads effortlessly into the erotics of Hardy's plot machinations. The act of writing serves, in Barthes's terms, to arouse 'an energy of seduction which no legal defence of the subject I fling upon the page can any longer halt'. Yet, as Barthes acknowledges, in a mercantile society 'one must end up with a work'; the writer must construct, as Hardy often recognized, 'a piece of merchandise'.[20] The split between an

ecstatic writing which recreates the moment and the market ne
sequential plotting seems to echo a split in the subject between perception and thought-process, a split which is both constituted in and
unravelled by writing. Thus when Owen and Cytherea flee the primal
scene in Hocbridge and take a train to the south coast, the linguistic
evocation of landscape possesses a distinctly erotic charge:

> They watched the undulating cornlands, monotonous to all their compan-
> ions; the stony and clayey prospect succeeding those, with its angular and
> abrupt hills. Boggy moors came next, now withered and dry—the spots
> upon which pools usually spread their waters showing themselves as
> circles of smooth bare soil, overrun by a network of innumerable little
> fissures (*DR*, p. 53).

Desire is topographically realized in the body, erogenous zones
defined and lines of force articulated through landscape description.
Immediately after this, when Cytherea sees her advertisement for a
governess-post in print, she experiences an alienation from the self
which had begun with the death of her father. ' "That can't be myself;
how odd I look!" she said, and smiled' (*DR*, p. 54). A proper name,
Derrida remarks, 'ought to have no meaning, ought to be a mere
reference'. But since 'it is caught up in the network of language, it
always begins to signify'.[21] Within the rhetoric of the novel, character
exists as signature, name or document: hollow pits, locked cabinets
and postal sacks tell stories. The heroine has entered the world of
exchange, becoming a commodity reified by the self-distantiation of
writing. Effectively, Owen Graye, who stands as surrogate father,
leads her within the economy of the narrative to Edward Springrove.

When she meets Springrove for the first time on the steamer at
Lulwind Cove, Cytherea acknowledges him instantly in a ludicrous
catalogue of misrecognitions:

> Raising her eyes from her feet, which, standing on the firm deck,
> demanded her attention no longer, she acquired perceptions of the
> newcomer in the following order: unknown waistcoat; unknown face. The
> man was not her brother, but a total stranger (*DR*, p. 62).

For a hero who is eventually to be pitted against the Byronic Manston,
Springrove evinces a remarkable bisexuality of feature. Although the
upper part of his face is 'handsomely formed' and of 'sufficiently
masculine regularity', the narrator suggests that 'his brows were
somewhat too softly arched and finely pencilled for one of his sex'
(*DR*, p. 63). The dislocation of sexual polarities into a changing pat-

tern of ambivalent dispositions and diverse corporeal pleasures is to become a persistent undertone in *Desperate Remedies*. The narrative voice appears curiously ambivalent in its tracing out of desire, able both to accept and reject the prevailingly patriarchal ethos which it describes. A number of narrative comments depend upon tacitly sexist assumptions for their interpretation. When brother and sister are thrown upon their own resources, for instance, it is claimed that the female's 'greater narrowness' of resource endows her with greater resilience (*DR*, p. 52); later on, the victimized Cytherea's interest in her wedding clothes is ascribed to the same feminine weakness. Yet there is a clearly betrayed unease with the very stereotypes to which Cytherea tries intermittently to mould herself. When she determines to marry Manston to help her brother, for instance, such 'heroic self-abnegation' is not endorsed by the narrator (*DR*, p. 255). The register of signs under which women are inscribed is markedly various, contradictory and self-deconstructing. In the plotting, Cytherea is offered pitifully little choice—Springrove, Manston or Miss Aldclyffe—and her final acceptance of the ineffectual Springrove leaves both reader and heroine uninvolved. This kind of alienation effect is typical of the creative uncertainties of Hardy's handling of gender issues, and continually undermines inherited conventions of textual decorum.

Such an undermining is implicit in the Edenic placidity of the rowing scenes in Budmouth Bay, where the glassy sea encloses a subterranean life which is radically other:

> The breeze had entirely died away, leaving the water of that rare glassy smoothness which is unmarked even by the small dimples of the least aërial movement. Purples and blues of divers shades were reflected from this mirror accordingly as each undulation sloped east or west. They could see the rocky bottom some twenty feet beneath them, luxuriant with weeds of various growths, and dotted with pulpy creatures reflecting a silvery and spangled radiance upwards to their eyes (*DR*, p. 80).

The flat surface which conceals difference mirrors the internalized divisions within the text and its rhetoric, where discourse and figuration, language and desire, endlessly mirror and mask each other. The monstrous zone of the strangely erotic 'pulpy creatures' corresponds to the region of that fluidity and play upon whose subjugation the construction of the male bourgeois subject seems to depend. The entwining seductions of that play, and the equally powerful demands of the controlling ego, combine to produce both the most potent figure in the novel, Aeneas Manston, and the oscillations of the narrative voice. The moment in the rowing-boat is marked by the onset of love and the simultaneous withdrawal of that love. While the ostensible reason for Springrove's embarrassment is the prior engagement to his cousin, such a Chekhovian hanging back is remarkably consistent with a splitting in the personality marked by the opening description of his physiognomy. Femininity, in either Springrove or Cytherea, is a subversive inscription within the uniform script of the bourgeois text.

A more overtly transgressive subversion is envisaged in the seduction-scene between Miss Aldclyffe and Cytherea, the daughter of her former lover. After looking in the mirror 'at the reflection of her own magnificent resources in face and bosom' (*DR*, p. 110), the younger Cytherea admits the older into her bed, the mistress flinging her arms round the young girl and pressing her 'gently to her heart' (*DR*, p. 122). Remarking upon their identity of name, Miss Aldclyffe pertinently demands of Cytherea, '"Why can't you kiss me as I can kiss you?"' (*DR*, p. 113). When she reveals through her prayers that she has a male admirer, Cytherea is pressed by Miss Aldclyffe: '"Cytherea, try to love me more than you love him—do. I love you more sincerely than any man can. Do, Cythie: don't let any man stand between us. O, I can't bear that!"' (*DR*, p. 115). Miss Aldclyffe's taste, like that of Knight and Angel Clare, is for 'an artless woman who had not been sullied by a man's lips' (*DR*, p. 116), but she complains that '"you can hardly find a girl whose heart has not been *had*—is not an old thing half worn out by some He or another"' (*DR*, p. 116). Men, in Miss Aldclyffe's account, are fickle in love: '"I shall never forget you for anybody else, as men do"' (*DR*, p. 118). While the mistress composes herself for sleep, the lady's maid (now promoted to 'companion') becomes possessed by the sound of the waterfall in the grounds of Knapwater House, accompanied by the creaking of the water-wheel. As Virginia Woolf remarked, 'perhaps the most remarkable quality in the book is the sound of a waterfall that echoes and booms through its pages'.[22] This sound produces a striking moment in which the inanimate and contingent spring into a preternatural life which crushes out consciousness:

> To imagine the inside of the engine-house, whence these noises pro-
> ceeded, was now a necessity. No window, but crevices in the door,
> through which, probably, the moon-beams streamed in the most attenu-
> ated and skeleton-like rays, striking sharply upon portions of wet rusty
> cranks and chains; a glistening wheel, turning incessantly, labouring in

the dark like a captive starving in a dungeon; and instead of a floor below, gurgling water, which on account of the darkness could only be heard; water which laboured up dark pipes almost to where she lay (*DR*, p. 120).

At the climax of this concatenation of sounds Cytherea hears a third noise, 'a very soft gurgle or rattle' (*DR*, p. 120), which is later revealed to be the death-rattle of Miss Aldclyffe's invisible father. Thus the relationship between the two Cythereas is sealed through the off-stage death of a second father.

This scene resonates with unconscious power, exploring as it does the issues of sexuality, gender and class, which entangle both novelist and audience. Miss Aldclyffe enters Cytherea's bedroom as of right, as mistress and landowner, and exerts her dominant class position for sexual ends. Only a little earlier Cytherea, oppressed by the 'petty, vulgar details of servitude', had desired to live like the sheep in the park (*DR*, p. 98), and there is something sheep-like in her passivity at such crucial junctures of the plot. Miss Aldclyffe is imagined as deviant because of her spinsterhood; she has ignored the economic imperative towards heterosexuality after her early unhappy encounters with men. Lesbianism is represented in the text in terms of marginalization through a parodic version of the mother–daughter relationship. The silencing of the voices of lesbianism in the period is inscribed in the very text which articulates a lesbian situation. A sexuality which is characteristically anti-phallic is sacrificed by the insertion into the plot of the notably phallic son/lover/husband, Aeneas Manston. As Jeffrey Weeks has shown, attitudes towards lesbian sexuality were overdetermined by

> The roles that society assigned women; the ideology which articulated, organised and regulated this; the dominant notions of female sexuality in the ideology; and the actual possibilities for the development by women of an autonomous sexuality.[23] → got this

Thus it is that 'deviant' sexuality is constructed within a legal and ideological relation to marriage, the family and procreation. Within such a society and such a discourse the feminine is that which is not masculine. The female genitalia must be rendered invisible, since in Lacanian terms the institution of meaning depends upon the sign of the phallus. Cytherea Aldclyffe's desperate search for, and employment of, her implacable son may be illuminated by Luce Irigaray's notion of the 'mother woman' as castrator. Such a figure 'continually undoes' man's work, 'creating an endless interval, game, agitation, or non-limit':

> But, for fear of leaving her a subject-life of her own, which would entail
> his sometimes being her locus and her thing, in a dynamic inter-subjective
> process, man remains within a master–slave dialectic. He is ultimately the
> slave of a God on whom he bestows the qualities of an absolute master.
> He is secretly a slave to the power of the mother woman, which he
> subdues or destroys.[24]

intro to the chapter

If the lesbian scene exposes one type of class-exploitation, it does so with a curious charge of excitation which derives from the author's own struggles with a 'mother woman'. As a boy, Hardy had been taken up by the mistress of the Kingston Maurward estate (Knapwater House), Julia Augusta Martin. According to his own account, Mrs Martin 'had grown passionately fond of Tommy almost from his infancy'. His regard for her was 'almost that of a lover', and she became accustomed to take him 'into her lap and kiss' him 'until he was quite a big child'. Hardy adds laconically, 'He quite reciprocated her fondness'.[25] Michael Millgate remarks that Hardy never forgot 'the woman who had overwhelmed him not only by her fond and flattering encouragement' but also by her 'voluptuousness of dress and person'.[26] This nexus of sexuality and class condescension fuels the lesbian scenes of *Desperate Remedies*. The young Hardy self-evidently saw Mrs Martin both as a substitute for his own lowly parentage and as an enticingly powerful lover who would take the initiative. Such patterns of behaviour were clearly identifiable in the economy of the 'family romance' delineated by Freud:

> the child's imagination becomes engaged in the task of getting free from
> the parents of whom he now has a low opinion and of replacing them by
> others, who, as a rule, are of higher social standing. He will make use in
> this connection of any opportune coincidences from his actual experience,
> such as his becoming acquainted with the Lord of the Manor or some
> landed proprietor if he lives in the country or with some member of the
> aristocracy if he lives in town. Chance occurrences of this kind arouse the
> child's envy, which finds expression in a phantasy in which both his
> parents are replaced by others of better birth.[27]

The scene between the two Cythereas disrupts, fragments and re-enacts psychoanalytic accounts of identity-formation. Cytherea Graye begins by contemplating her own image in the mirror; she is then joined in bed by another who is also the same, the older Cytherea. Simultaneously with this scene of passion, the older Cytherea's father dies, just as the younger Cytherea's father, Miss Aldclyffe's former lover, had died at the outset of the story. According to Jacques Lacan, the speaking subject only comes into existence through repression of the desire for the lost mother: to be enabled to speak is also to experience lack, to enter into the patriarchally organized symbolic order. Near the beginning of its life, the child enters into the mirror stage which imbues it with a sense of unitary identity and enables it to inhabit the imaginary, a dyadic mother–child relationship dominated by the maternal body. The mirror stage establishes the objectifying nature of any kind of reflexive access to the self, prior to the subject's entry into inter-subjective relations. Irigaray has written strikingly of the strange dialectic that is involved:

> You look at yourself in the mirror. And your mother is already there. And soon your daughter [as] mother. Between the two what are you?. . . Just a scansion: the time when one becomes the other. . . Only this liquid which leaves one and arrives in the other, and which has no name.[28]

Cytherea's ego is constituted on the basis of its specular counterpart; the Lacanian imaginary is fundamentally narcissistic—Cytherea loves Cytherea—and is characterized by an act of misrecognition. Detachment from the source of infantile satisfaction is completed when the subject finds her place within a signifying system. As Lacan strikingly expresses it,

> the symbol manifests itself first of all as the murder of the thing, and this death constitutes in the subject the eternalisation of his desire.[29]

The giving of meaning entails division: the individual subject is produced through language so as to conform to the pre-existent symbolic order. As the subject enters the symbolic realm the repression entailed creates an anarchic under-language of the unconscious. The subject, in this account, must find herself within an enabling symbolic order dominated by the name-of-the-father. Language is always other than the speaking subject who enters into it through the operation of the castration complex. The child discerns that the mother lacks the phallus and this observation serves to insert the child into the field of sexual difference. Lacan insists, of course, that the phallus is not the penis, but rather a simulacrum of that organ. In this regard, it is no coincidence that in the opening of the narrative, Mr Graye is working on the 'upper part of a neighbouring church spire', the top of which is visible to Cytherea's 'idling eyes' (*DR*, p. 45) as they play upon this 'new erection' (*DR*, p. 46). In the Lacanian scheme the phallus is the signifier of desire which enables meanings to be produced. Prior to the subject's entry into the phallic symbolic order the mother is the recipient of all emotional demands, the source of all satisfaction. The uncovering of the 'fact' of castration detaches the subject from her dependence upon the mother and situates her in culture; the dyadic mother–child relationship is complicated by triangulation when the father comes upon the scene, a triangulation which induces splitting and triggers off the workings of the unconscious. Recognition of the father is the recognition of difference: the subject is what she is only by excluding another. The seduction scene valorizes the imaginary along lines which are predicated in Laura Mulvey's re-reading of Lacan. Mulvey argues that the function of woman in the formation of the patriarchal unconscious is twofold. First, she 'symbolises the castration threat by her real lack of a penis', and secondly, through this absence, 'raises her child into the symbolic'. Once this is achieved, the woman's 'meaning' is at an end: 'It does not last into the world of law and language except as a memory which oscillates between memory of maternal plenitude and memory of lack'. Miss Aldclyffe's relationships with Manston and Cytherea, her surrogate daughter, uncannily act out the theoretical position sketched by Mulvey:

> She turns her child into the signifier of her own desire to possess a penis (the condition, she imagines, of entry into the symbolic). Either she must gracefully give way to the word, the name of the father and the law, or else struggle to keep her child down with her in the half-light of the imaginary.[30]

The figure of the woman, in such an economy, stands as 'signifier for the male other', 'bound by a symbolic order in which man can live out his fantasies and obsessions through linguistic command'.[31] So it is that, at the interview for the post of steward, Miss Aldclyffe sits in the window recess, 'wearing her veil down', as she eagerly appoints her son as overseer to the estate (*DR*, p. 142). But if it is ostensibly the woman who inhabits this 'half-light of the imaginary' in terms of plot, the narrator also remains most characteristically concealed. Many years later, anticipating a dramatized performance of extracts from *The Dynasts* at Oxford, Hardy asked to be placed 'in some obscure box or (failing that) behind in the wings, from which I can come out at any time without notice'.[32] The hidden author relates to the voyeuristic elements in his own narrative, to the veiled situation of the woman, and to the mastery of author and reader in a posture of domi-

nant specularity. It is part of the pleasurable unevenness of the text in
Desperate Remedies that such mastery can be disrupted; but the author
as voyeur is always reinstated by such disruptions.

The child's banishment from the unitary plenitude of the maternal
body into the anxieties of sexual difference is sensationally enacted in
Cytherea's experiences at Knapwater House. One striking incident
before the bedroom scene anticipates the psychic movement of the
text. It comes at the end of a quarrel between the two women:

> Cytherea, red and panting, took up her candlestick and advanced to the
> table to get a light. As she stood close to them the rays from the candles
> struck sharply on her face. She usually bore a much stronger likeness to
> her mother than to her father, but now, looking with a grave, reckless,
> and angered expression of countenance at the kindling wick as she held it
> slanting into the other flame, her father's features were distinct in her
> (*DR*, p. 107).

Such a passage, with its sensationalist evocation of the 'red and pant-
ing' daughter taking up the candlestick and acquiring thereby traces of
the paternal physiognomy, is characteristic of the textual qualities of
Desperate Remedies. The 'father's features' which are cancelled out in
the ludicrously apposite deaths of Mr Graye and Mr Aldclyffe, and
held at bay in the luxurious entwining of the female bodies, reappear
with a vengeance in the eruption into the action of that 'voluptuary
with activity' (*DR*, p. 143), Aeneas Manston, a symbolic father whose
power obliterates the biological fathers, the brotherly protection of
Owen Graye and the rivalry of Edward Springrove.

Cytherea first glimpses Manston in a thunderstorm, as she is passing
the old manor house. He is 'dark in outline' and 'of towering height',
and she feels that his eyes are 'going through' her (*DR*, p. 162).
Inviting her into the house to shelter, he points to 'a round wet spot as
large as a nasturtium leaf, which had suddenly appeared upon the
white surface of the step' (*DR*, p. 163), in an image which perilously
synthesizes naturalistic observation and sexual excitation. As the two
shelter in the porch their clothing touches, a momentary contact which
sends 'a thrill through Cytherea' (*DR*, p. 164). Stepping inside the
house, she discovers that the only article of furniture yet unpacked is
an organ. With a hilarious ignorance of readerly decorum, Hardy
allows the phallically imposing Manston to assure the heroine, '"You
would soon acquire the touch for an organ"' (*DR*, p. 165). In the
midst of the thunderstorm the steward begins to play:

Cytherea had never heard music in the completeness of full orchestral
power, and the tones of the organ, which reverberated with considerable
effect in the comparatively small space of the room, heightened by the
elemental strife of light and sound outside, moved her to a degree out of
proportion to the actual power of the mere notes, practised as was the
hand that produced them. The varying strains—now loud, now soft;
simple, complicated, weird, touching, grand, boisterous, subdued; each
phase distinct, yet modulating into the next with a graceful and easy
flow—shook and bent her to themselves, as a gushing brook shakes and
bends a shadow cast across its surface (*DR*, p. 167).

Enslaved by the organ, Cytherea is 'swayed into emotional opinions
concerning the strange man before her'. New impulses enter into her
'with a gnawing thrill', and she finds herself 'involuntarily shrinking
up' beside Manston, 'looking with parted lips at his face'. As the storm
abates, she draws a 'long breath of relief' (*DR*, p. 168). By the end of
this sequence the heroine has become, in her own mind, an object of
male desire:

'O, how is it that man has so fascinated me?' was all she could think. Her
own self, as she had sat spell-bound before him, was all she could see.
Her gait was constrained, from the knowledge that his eyes were upon her
until she had passed the hollow by the waterfall, and by ascending the rise
had become hidden from his view by the boughs of the overhanging trees
(*DR*, p. 169).

In imagination Manston's black eyes seem to be 'piercing her again'
(*DR*, p. 169), and she is fearfully entranced by his 'marvellous
beauty' (*DR*, p. 172). The disturbance in the writing here marks the
decisive break in the heroine's career: she seems to emerge from the
imaginary into the symbolic. The realm of the imaginary, close to the
body, is passionately inhabited by the two Cythereas in the bedroom
scene. The symbolic disrupts this duality with a new form of phallically dominated relationship.

Juliet MacCannell's analysis of Lacan describes how emergence into
the symbolic effects the entry into struggle and work in a movement
which reproduces the Hegelian master–slave relationship:

The imaginary, in which opinion and value are the key components,
ceases to function properly in the structure of mastery: the master enters
into the relationship purely for prestige and at the risk of his life.[33]

Manston enters into the stewardship of Knapwater in precisely this
spirit of risk-taking. His filial relationship to Miss Aldclyffe, and his
apparently bigamous intentions towards Cytherea, are equally to

remain hidden. He exerts power of mastery over both women; whilst ostensibly in Miss Aldclyffe's employ, it is she who adopts the slave-like posture:

> The slave, now a worker, submits not to the passion for prestige of the master, but to the law, the law that he is to satisfy the *desire and enjoyment* of the other.[34]

The passions of the imaginary are, in MacCannell's account, 'so many *cul de sacs*', and the *sac* in Lacan's terminology 'is an image of the coming of the Symbolic' by which the adult is enslaved. She goes on:

> Passions, for Lacan, are the passions of the ego; they are superseded only by the advent of the Symbolic. The Symbolic replaces the indexical topography of the body with the iconic imagery of geometry, the graph, the number, etc. Images displace, replace, the body, but their provenance is from the body: we take a feature, a trait, the surface of the skin. From there we move to the idea of the skin as a covering, and from there to that of a sack.[35]

In his death-cell confession Manston recounts how, having murdered his wife Eunice, he placed her body in a sack and pushed it into the old oven in the outhouse. He later scatters some bones into the embers of the burning inn. At the crisis of the action the steward, observed in turn by Anne Seaway, Miss Aldclyffe and the detective hired by Mr Raunham, carries the female body in its sack to the pit and buries it. In contrast to this secret, enclosed covering, the narrator notes elsewhere how it is Miss Aldclyffe's custom, 'nourished by her own exclusiveness', to unlock the post-bag every day (*DR*, p. 185). Even in death, and beyond, Manston wields, through the power of his pen, the authority of the name-of-the-father. He acts throughout as an agent of the Oedipal, his very name identifying both his masculinity and his oppressive weight. Seated at the organ, Manston privileges self above otherness and identity over difference. Yet the notes of the organ are produced by air, just as the voice depends upon that systematic articulation of signs which constitutes a language. Manston's claim to an originary selfhood, his role of the Lacanian son as father, is continually threatened and dispersed by the play of difference, as in the moment when he gazes into the rainwater-butt:

> Staves of sunlight slanted down through the still pool, lighting it up with wonderful distinctness. Hundreds of thousands of minute living creatures sported and tumbled in its depth with every contortion that gaiety could suggest; perfectly happy, though consisting only of a head, or a tail, or at

most a head and a tail, and all doomed to die within the twenty-four hours (*DR*, p. 244).

Manston with uncharacteristic banality reads this as an emblem of the brevity of life: ' "Damn my position! Why shouldn't I be happy through my little day too?" ', and determines to pursue the 'invulnerable Nobody', Cytherea (*DR*, p. 244). The sport of the minute creatures also suggests the dissolution of that fixed identity to which the phallic male is so implacably wedded as a lawgiver who both instigates and represses desire. Here are no individual identities, but rather a dissolution of selfhood into molecular particles. As Manston stares into the butt the reader experiences a vertiginous real-ization that to be human is to be both one and many, aggregative and dispersed; language decreates personality, leaving the reader in con-templation of a state of being which is fluid and migratory.

The introduction of Aeneas Manston into the Knapwater Estate by Miss Aldclyffe disrupts the narrative tone through the intensity of the Oedipal drama. Indeed, a form of incestuous flirtation is inherent in the steward's reaction to his employer's partiality:

> His previous experience of the effect of his form and features upon womankind *en masse*, had taught him to flatter himself that he could account by the same law of natural selection for the extraordinary interest Miss Aldclyffe had hitherto taken in him, as an unmarried man (*DR*, p. 191).

The attraction between villain and heroine is similarly more frantic and more deadly than the pallid love-affair at Budmouth which is easily suspended because of Springrove's engagement to his cousin, Adelaide Hinton, a character later destined to marry, in Farmer Bollens, a man 'old enough to be her father' (*DR*, p. 267). As both son and lover, Manston is devoted to the project of seduction which triggers the plot. The complex of infantile fear and sadism which fuels Cytherea's pre-marital dream acts as an over-compensation for her desire for this father with his 'scorching white heat' (*DR*, p. 248):

> During the dilemma she fell into a troubled sleep, and dreamt that she was being whipped with dry bones suspended on strings, which rattled at every blow like those of a malefactor on a gibbet; that she shifted and shrank and avoided every blow, and they fell then upon the wall to which she was tied. She could not see the face of the executioner for his mask, but his form was like Manston's (*DR*, pp. 263-64).

The rational explanation—the sounds are created by icicles weighing down the branches outside her window—does nothing to overlay or mask the transgressive potential of Manston; an illegitimate and unacknowledged heir, he is associated with social resentment and subversion of familial order. Manston's avenging imperviosity seems to embody the patriarchal law otherwise absent from the fatherless text; his libidinous eroticism, on the other hand, threatens to overturn that law. Lacan noted the paradox by which 'the ravaging effects of the paternal figure are to be observed with particular frequency where the father really has the function of a legislator'. Such a figure, when he 'poses as the pillar of the faith, as a paragon of integrity and devotion', is furnished 'with all too many opportunities of being in a posture of undeserving, inadequacy, even of fraud'—a posture which succeeds in 'excluding the Name-of-the-Father from its position in the signifier'.[36] Narrative resolution demands that such a challenge to order be contained, and it is this requirement which leads to the weaving of the detective plot and the virtual eclipse of the heroine in the later stretches of the novel.

The destruction of the family unit in *Desperate Remedies* is symptomatic of a crisis provided by new modes of production which locate power outside that unit. Within the rural narrative these modes are represented by the railway's eruption into Wessex. In describing the 'many-gabled, medieval building' of the Three Tranters, Hardy indicates how the old coaching inn has been rendered obsolete, the 'stream of traffic' having been 'absorbed' by the building of the railway (*DR*, p. 153). The decaying outbuildings stand as witness with the 'general stillness' (*DR*, p. 153) to these new processes; the voices of the workfolk in the ensuing cider-making scene articulate that historical displacement. Under the supervision of the farming landlord, Edward Springrove's father, a group of workfolk are putting crushed apples into bags. Hardy provides a detailed description of the worker's accoutrements, but identifies only Mr Springrove, Richard Crickett the parish-clerk, and Gad Weedy, Springrove's 'man'. The remainder of the work-force are categorized as 'brown-faced peasants' who wear 'smock-frocks' (*DR*, p. 155). They discuss the enigmatic new steward and the uncertain temper of his employer. The conversation turns more general, Hardy taking pains to reproduce in this section of the novel a literary version of Dorset dialect speech:

> 'Clerk Crickett, I fancy you know everything about everybody', said Gad.
> 'Well so's', said the clerk modestly. 'I do know a little. It comes to me.'

'And I know where from.'

'Ah.'

'That wife o' thine. She's an entertainen woman, not to speak disrespectful.'

'She is: and a winnen one. Look at the husbands she've had—God bless her.'

'I wonder you could stand third in that list, Clerk Crickett', said Mr Springrove.

'Well, 't has been a power o' marvel to myself oftentimes. Yes, matrimony do begin wi' "Dearly beloved", and ends wi' "Amazement", as the prayer-book says. But what could I do, neighbour Springrove? 'Twas ordained to be.' (*DR*, pp. 156-57).

Cytherea's arrival on the scene is greeted with a silent gaze, the farmer apologizes 'for detaining by his cider-making any well-dressed woman' (*DR*, p. 158), though prior to her arrival Clerk Crickett has dismissed her as one who ' "han't a stick o' furniture to call her own" ' (*DR*, pp. 157-58). When Cytherea withdraws, Weedy reflects that ' "by the tongue of her" ' she ' "didn't take her degrees in our country" ' (*DR*, p. 159), whilst Farmer Springrove assures her, ' "the Inn and I seem almost a pair of fossils" ' (*DR*, p. 160).

In such a scene the text unconsciously exposes its own inequalities; the dialogue between classes (and here the lady's companion stands in somewhat uncomfortably for her employer) is essentially antagonistic. *Desperate Remedies*, composed prior to Hardy's invention of Wessex, already registers the displacement of the workfolk and their regional dialect by the metropolitan centre. A standardized system of orthography and pronunciation was necessary for the formation of the capitalist enterprise. The bourgeois class, in *Desperate Remedies* and elsewhere, experiences language as its own possession. The introduction of a formalized dialect speech signals inferiority inscribed as comedy. Yet Hardy, even in this early exercise when he is 'feeling his way to a method', as he put it in the 1889 Preface, is scrupulous in recording the minute gradations of the rural economy. Farmer Springrove seems to exemplify the harmonious relations between employer and labourer, but in the cider-making that harmony is overshadowed by the presence of the landed class. As Raymond Williams observed, on his way to school the young Hardy would 'see the mansion of Kingston Maurward. . . on which his father did some of the estate work, and this showed a sudden difference of degree'. As a writer, Williams adds, Hardy is 'neither owner nor tenant, dealer nor labourer, but an observer and chronicler'.[37] The problem for the beginning author in *Desperate Remedies* is both to insert himself into the institution of writing and to raise himself up the social ladder. Hardy's own ambivalent class position is implicated in the speech patterns of both rustic and middle-class characters. In the cider-making scene he demonstrates how the rural economy works through co-operative enterprise and linguistic equality. The author brings his working people briefly to life, only to destroy that way of life in the fire and abandon them in favour of the higher-class protagonists.

The connection between the Promethean Manston and the inroads of the railway is made manifest in the striking scene when the steward, walking in the woods, comes across the railway cutting:

> A sudden rattle on his right hand caused him to start from his reverie, and turn in that direction. There, before him, he saw rise up from among the trees a fountain of sparks and smoke, then a red glare of light coming forward towards him; then a flashing panorama of illuminated oblong pictures; then the old darkness, more impressive than ever (*DR*, p. 176).

Such a moment, while it works to forward the plot (this is the very train upon which his wife will arrive), also dramatizes the way Wessex is changing; the 'old darkness' can never be the same again. If it is true, as George Wotton argues, that there is 'no awareness in Hardy's writing of the possibilities for working-class solidarity',[38] that is partly because of the author's clear-sighted recognition of audience expectations and the needs of the literary market, and it is that recognition which transforms *Desperate Remedies* into a novel of sensation and detection in its later stages.

The vogue for detective fiction, Clive Bloom argues, formed a bridge between romanticism and modernism. The characterless characters are a sign of the modernist self 'abstracted from itself', 'absorbed in watching its own processes of creation'.[39] The shaping of narrative in this genre 'abolished subject matter in favour of form', and thus the story 'is not the tale of the teller but of the reader'; it is 'a continuing tale of what it means to read'.[40] In such fiction, Bloom argues, 'the "repressed" is already known to the culprit and to the victim', and the culprits 'leave *clues* because they wish to leave clues'—Manston's poem to Eunice, for instance:

> As a projection of various signs the victim is re-constructed in the mind of the analyst in order for a final deduction to be made. The deduction concerns the crime *not* the criminal. The criminal then becomes another sign, another clue, rather than a resolution of all clues gathered within his

personality. In the classic detective tale the criminal always wishes to be caught.[41]

Bloom's argument that, in taking up the roles of detective and culprit, characters acknowledge bonds of mutual dependence, illuminates the curiously symbiotic relationship between Springrove and Manston. Both men become relatively emptied of content in the later reaches of the novel, where the formal requirements of the sensation novel predominate. Bloom also observes the sacrificial nature of the victim, 'worthless, unremarked, a necessary yet inconsequential sacrifice';[42] in vindicating himself to Miss Aldclyffe, Manston dismisses his wife Eunice as a 'third-rate actress' (*DR*, p. 189). For the reader of *Desperate Remedies*, it is the figure of Manston which resonates, Springrove remaining a cipher. As Bloom remarks, in detective fiction the criminal is both 'artist and text', whilst the detective figure is 'merely a reader':

> The criminal/artist forgets himself in his act (murder/the art creation) and extinguishes his personality by putting it *all* in the service of the act. Nevertheless, the act, the murder, the artistic creation embody him and encapsulate, as in amber, a memorial to the murderer/artist's presence. . . Murder/art reconstructs the subject through a testimonial which acts as the *text's* (the deed's) *memory*.[43]

In his 'Last Words' Manston expounds the true narrative for which Springrove, Owen Graye and Mr Raunham's detective had sought, in a conventional document which Bloom characterizes as 'a final signature to the original deed, the original creative act'.[44] In the moment of apprehension, Bloom writes, the culprit confirms the presence and identity of his pursuer; he 'looks into the eyes of the detective as into a mirror'.[45] When Springrove jumps through the window to rescue Cytherea from Manston's clutches, the narrative, fully caught up in the register of melodrama, records that a 'fiery glance on the one side, a glance of pitiless justice on the other, passed between them' (*DR*, p. 398). Such a confrontation leads to the resolution, in Bloom's account: 'Having given himself away the culprit awaits his reward, which is the hangman's noose upon another stage, while the detective pockets the loot'.[46] In Springrove's case the loot turns out to be Cytherea. Bloom's analysis accurately registers the final reduction, in detective fiction, of the culprit to corpse-like immobility: Manston's demonic energies are ultimately to be contained in the 'very plain box' which is carried through Casterbridge to the gaol (*DR*, p. 401), and

his unwitting accomplice, Miss Aldclyffe, almost immediately afterwards dies of an 'effusion' (*DR*, p. 413).

The literature of detection is inextricably urban in character, and
some of the most surprising moments in the later reaches of *Desperate
Remedies* arise out of the characters' immersion in the lower-class
environs of the metropolis. Thus, Edward Springrove, searching for
evidence of Manston's marriage, is introduced to the living-room of
Mrs Higgins, in a Dickensian scene of squalid energies:

> A roll of baby-linen lay on the floor; beside it a pap-clogged spoon and an
> overturned tin pap-cup. Against the wall a Dutch clock was fixed out of
> level, and ticked wildly in longs and shorts, its entrails hanging down
> beneath its white face and wiry hands, like the faeces of a Harpy. . . . A
> baby was crying against every chair-leg, the whole family of six or seven
> being small enough to be covered by a washing-tub (*DR*, p. 332).

This glimpse of proletarian poverty serves only as backdrop to
Springrove's discovery of Manston's poetic effusion, and the young
architect hastens off to the Charing Cross post-office secretly observed
by the steward. Having ascertained the time that Springrove's package
will arrive at Tolchurch the next morning, Manston idles 'about the
streets and over the river' (*DR*, p. 335).

At this slack moment of unfocused urban peregrination the narrator
introduces one of the most remarkable passages in the novel, a para-
graph which echoes and presages some of the most intimate concerns
of modernism:

> Thus, amid his concentration did Manston receive perceptions of the
> individuals about him in the lively thoroughfare of the Strand; tall men
> looking insignificant; little men looking great and profound; lost women
> of miserable repute looking as happy as the days are long; wives, happy
> by assumption, looking careworn and miserable. Each and all were alike
> in this one respect, that they followed a solitary trail like the inwoven
> threads which form a banner, and all were equally unconscious of the
> significant whole they collectively showed forth (*DR*, pp. 335-36).

On the social level the scene projects that sense of the imprisonment of
the self and imperviousness to outer view of which Cytherea has
already complained to Owen. She tells her brother how difficult it is
'to adjust our outer and inner life', and urges the point that the
dismissive pity of others was a 'whole life' to her, ' "as full of hours,
minutes, and peculiar minutes, of hopes and dreads, smiles, whisper-
ings, tears, as theirs" '. Nobody, she concludes, ' "can enter into
another's nature truly, that's what is so grievous" ' (*DR*, pp. 272-73).

A similar conjunction of feeling is encompassed by Hardy's earlier poem, 'She to Him, II', where the speaker, reflecting on how she will be slightingly recalled by a lover after her death, asserts,

> . . . your thin thought, in two small words conveyed,
> Was no such fleeting phantom-thought to me,
> But the Whole Life wherein my part was played (*CP*, p. 15).

Loss of individuality within the metropolitan crowd was often sensed in the writing of the period. In 'The Lions in Trafalgar Square', for instance, Richard Jefferies recorded a similar moment:

> The roar of the rolling wheels sinks and becomes distant as the sound of a waterfall when dreams are coming. All abundant life is smooth and levelled, the abruptness of the individuals lost in the flowing current like separate flowers drawn along in a border, like music heard so far off that the notes are molten and the theme only remains.[47]

A significant frame for Manston's reflections at this juncture is offered by Walter Benjamin's observation that the 'original social content of the detective story was the obliteration of the individual's traces in the big-city crowd'.[48] Hardy transforms his villain here into a *flâneur* who observes the 'unconscious' collectivity in a movement which recalls Engels's description of the London crowd cited by Benjamin. Engels finds that 'these Londoners have been forced to sacrifice the best qualities of their human nature' in the transformation into the urban mass. They are all 'human beings with the same qualities and powers', yet they 'crowd by one another as though they had nothing in common'.[49] Years later Hardy was to reflect that London 'appears not to *see itself*':

> Each individual is conscious of *himself*, but nobody conscious of themselves collectively, except perhaps some poor gaper who stares round with a half-idiotic aspect.[50]

This mass comprises, for Manston, 'inwoven threads which form a banner' (*DR*, p. 366), and for Benjamin, 'the agitated veil' through which he saw Paris; the image of the crowd tentatively evoked by Hardy's text becomes a constitutive image of expressionist alienation for modernism, and is ultimately to be realized visually in such films as Lang's *Metropolis* or Widor's *The Crowd*. Yet these 'threads' are formed out of a 'solitary trail'; the mark of the crowd is a loneliness and separation which, as Benjamin puts it, 'penetrates the disappearing person like a pigment'.[51] The transformation, in the authorial vision, of individuals who are variously 'insignificant', 'profound', 'happy' or 'careworn and miserable' (*DR*, p. 336) into the unconscious collectivity is accounted for, in Benjamin's reflections, by the Marxist analysis of capitalist production, in which workers 'learn to co-ordinate their own movements to the uniform and unceasing motion of an automaton'.[52] Thus the shock of the human observer newly encountering the great metropolitan crowds corresponds to the factory workers' immolation to the machine.

John Rignall has argued that the *flâneur* is 'at once an observed historical phenomenon, a type among the inhabitants of nineteenth-century Paris, the representation of a way of experiencing metropolitan life, a literary motif, and an image of the commodity in its relation to the crowd'.[53] Many of these elements are discernible in Hardy's treatment of Manston's vision in London. The villain's act of perception bears out Rignall's contention that the characteristic emphasis in the literature of the *flâneur* is upon the gaze, and that there are 'affinities between this complex form of seeing in the city and the practice of nineteenth-century realism'.[54] The position of Manston in this case becomes a paradigm of the narrator's stance as he performs what Rignall designates 'a dialectically double action of revelation and mystification'.[55] That the posited equivalence of seeing to knowing is inherently unstable, and would ultimately undermine the premises of realism, is borne out by the clashing narrative trajectories imbricated within the text of *Desperate Remedies*. The novel challenges its reader's hermeneutic skills just as the *flâneur* vainly seeks 'to attach meanings to the unfathomable face of the man of the crowd'.[56] In this sense Manston, like the *flâneur* in Poe or Baudelaire, deconstructs the epistemology of realism, and the text within which he exists balances precariously between realist and modernist procedure. Such writing potently diagnoses metamorphoses in both literary and social history. It is symptomatic, for instance, that Manston should be pursued to London by Springrove, whilst Cytherea is rendered increasingly invisible by the drama of pursuit and detection. The constituent image repertoire of modernity—the city-scape, the shock of the crowd—is encapsulated in the experience of the specifically male *flâneur*, women being typically excluded from the arena of public life by the patriarchal separation of spheres.[57]

The *flâneur*'s 'solitary dispossession' in his drifting absence of mind leads him, as Terry Eagleton notes, into a type of commodification:

Strolling self-composedly through the city, loitering without intent, lan-
guid yet secretly vigilant, he displays in living motion something of the
commodity's self-contradictory form.[58]

Manston's relationship to the crowd here is precisely that of
'complicity and contempt',[59] and he is reduced, in this unimportant
seminal moment of the text's self-forgetfulness, to an integer. It is a
movement which replicates the posture of the writer himself; writing,
according to Eagleton, 'scoops out the organic interiority of the
bourgeois-humanist subject: the very act whereby the subject
designates itself in the signifying chain is no more than a perpetual
standing-in for its own absence'.[60] The streets of London become, in
this moment, precisely an image of that 'labyrinth' into which
Cytherea steps on the death of her father (*DR*, p. 45), an image which
may be linked with Benjamin's childish quest through the 'Hohen-
zollern labyrinth' of Berlin.[61] The connection of the Hardyan crowd
and the observant *flâneur* becomes a figure of what Ned Lukacher
designates 'the search for the dialectical images buried deep within the
language of an epoch'.[62] The notion of burial is crucial to Benjamin's
project, which centres upon the retrieval of a buried past. He observes
that for 'successful excavations' what is indispensable to the 'dark joy
of the place of the finding' is the 'cautious probing of the spade in the
dark loam'.[63] It is this dark joy which the reader experiences through
Anne Seaway as she listens to the 'crunch of the steward's spade, as it
cut into the soft vegetable mould' (*DR*, p. 387) of the primal pit in
which he deposits his wife's body. The rapt quality of the language
here contrasts oddly with the dead hand of Hardy's prose at the climax
of the plot when Springrove confronts Manston. It is as if the
imagined labyrinthine burrowing possesses what Lukacher identifies
as the 'sexual dimension' to Benjamin's 'penchant for dark passage-
ways'.[64] The pit, situated 'midway between the waterfall and the
engine-house', serves as both maternal and sexual site at the climax of
the action, and the narrator remarks how the leaves have fallen into
'one fibrous mass' which is displaced by Manston's phallic spade in an
act simultaneously observed by his mother, his mistress and the detective (*DR*, p. 387). In arguing that 'everything satanic points down
into the depths of the earth', Benjamin cites Andreas Tscherning:
' "Whosoever knows me not will recognize me from my attitude. I
turn my eyes ever to the ground, because I once sprung from the
earth, and so I now look only on my mother" '.[65] Manston seeks both
the maternal womb and the buried self, and his frenzied digging might

be framed by another of Benjamin's observations:

> Language shows clearly that memory is not an instrument for exploring
> the past but its theatre. It is the medium of past experience, as the ground
> is the medium in which old cities lie interred. He who seeks to approach
> his own buried past must conduct himself like a man digging. . . . He
> must not be afraid to return again and again to the same matter; to scatter it
> as one scatters earth, to turn it over as one turns over soil.[66]

Thus will Hardy the writer return again and again to the soil of
Wessex in the course of his unrealizable project of attempting to
preserve for his own satisfaction 'a fairly true record of a vanishing
life', as he put it in the General Preface of 1912.

Like Benjamin, but more locally, Hardy felt compelled to sift
through the rubble of the past, a rubble which both dictated and
blocked his role as storyteller. Manston's digging may represent a
frenzied attempt to reconstitute the past, but the trajectory of his anti-
heroic career, his lack of a meaningful personal history, progressively
eliminates any such attempt. In *Desperate Remedies*, that is to say,
Hardy excavates the archaeological realist past of the novel in the very
act of fragmenting that tradition. The text celebrates the necessity and
impossibility of memory for the telling of a story. In Benjamin's
analysis of the art of the storyteller, reminiscence is the essence of
story, since it operates by creating 'the chain of tradition which passes
a happening on from generation to generation', and this is opposed to
the 'perpetuating remembrance' of the novelist.[67] *Desperate Remedies*
lies athwart literary history, signalling as it does a denaturalizing of
realist conventions and exploring the growing impossibility of
community in the displacement of the cider-making fraternity by the
individualistic Manston. The group of workers at the Three Tranters
functions as a community. As Benjamin remarks, 'A man listening to
a story is in the company of the story-teller'. The reader of the novel,
on the other hand, 'is isolated, more so than any other reader'.[68] It is
precisely the gift of listening which has disappeared. Hardy symptomatically records (in the disjointed plot, the galvanic characterization and the strange excursion into the metropolis of his first
marketable novel) that fading of sequentially conceived and reported
community (*Erfahrung*) under the impress of a modernist temporality
of unique, fragmented moments (*Erlebnis*) which occur outside community. 'The shock-experience the passer-by has in the crowd,
corresponds to what the worker experiences at his machine.'[69] The
fragmentation attributed here by Benjamin to the machine, and repre-

sented in Hardy's text by fire and railway, possesses its own kind of haunting beauty, but it is a beauty of fracture and loss. The destruction of the Three Tranters mirrors Benjamin's account of the novel-reader's addictive consumption of the text. The reader is ready to make the novel 'completely his own, to devour it, as it were':

> Indeed, he destroys, he swallows up the material as the fire devours logs in the fireplace. The suspense which permeates the novel is very much like the draught which stimulates the flame in the fireplace and enlivens its play. It is a dry material on which the burning interest of the reader feeds.[70]

The fires which rage through so many properties in realist fiction and naturalist drama appear to issue out of an authorial desire radically to alter, but not revolutionize, the social fabric. But such scenes also register and mimic the activity of readers or spectators consuming what is placed before them in the literary market. The meaningful identification of the individual with society which motivates the most characteristic fiction of the nineteenth century comes apart at the seams in a text like *Desperate Remedies*, one which problematizes the conception of a unified subject and of continuous temporal process in its schizophrenic treatment of women. The coincidence of individual and social experience which informs canonical early Hardy texts such as *Under the Greenwood Tree* or *Far From the Madding Crowd* is here intriguingly absent. That split between an existential subjectivity and an objectified social realm which often characterizes the work of the modernists is already visible here. The disturbed textuality of *Desperate Remedies* works to reveal the convention of realism as an effect of language, rather than vice versa. The novel deals with matters—sexuality, lesbianism, illegitimacy, bigamy, murder—which trouble the realist surface. In this respect, Hardy's first published novel might be described as one of realism's limit-texts, one of those works in which the arbitrariness of the sign is made distinctly visible to the reader. The author seems, with a naive independence, capable of throwing off the oppressive weight of verisimilitude in favour of a sensationally conceived, and formulaically executed, quest for homogeneity and significance.

    Benjamin's diagrammatic representation of his own life in the form of a labyrinth, characteristically mislaid, epitomizes the quest and its necessary failure. As Lukacher puts it:

It is because of this fundamental concealment, this insurmountable spell, that the structure of historical understanding for Benjamin is always allegorical; that is, fragmentary, deferred. Meaning and truth are always elsewhere; the act of interpretation is always suspended by an otherness it can never account for.[71]

Hardy was destined always to be a beginning writer, perpetually 'feeling his way to a method', and his dilemma is mirrored in the return of Manston from metropolitan crowd to primal pit. The image of the labyrinth which Cytherea enters at the outset combines with that of the 'solitary trail' (*DR*, p. 336) of Londoners to produce an impasse which can only be resolved by a return to the undifferentiated maternal space where all tensions are resolved. Such a faked resolution of contradictions in the text is brought about in the limp 'Sequel' which attaches itself as a supplement to the narrative. Here the renovation of the Carriford bells which celebrate Springrove's final espousal of Cytherea serves as emblem of a comic resolution which is denied by a tepidly compulsive repetition of the Budmouth sequence: Cytherea, in 'airy fairy dress', and Springrove in 'black stereotype raiment' (*DR*, p. 419), indulge in 'one half-minute's row' on Knapwater Lake as they pallidly attempt to renovate their earlier passion (*DR*, p. 420).

Hardy's substitution of an ornamental lake for the sea subverts the moment of comic closure and confirms the reader's impression that it is the death of Manston which terminates both past and text. Manston's 'Last Words' mechanically fulfil the prescriptive demands of detective fiction, but their manufactured quality is exploded by the villain's final reflection:

> I am now about to enter on my normal condition. For people are almost always in their graves. When we survey the long race of men, it is strange and still more strange to find that they are mainly dead men, who have scarcely ever been otherwise (*DR*, p. 407).

At last the disruptive son, lover and husband is about to revert to a single identity. Manston's 'Last Words', which are never truly his to possess, account for everything and explain nothing; they are wholly transparent and utterly opaque, leaving the reader's status unquestioned and discomposed. What is exposed is precisely that which remains most deeply hidden, the 'imbecility' of realism being premissed upon a falsely objective idea of the act of seeing. These last words, in which Manston contemplates the 'long race of men' who have 'scarcely ever been otherwise' than dead (*DR*, p. 407), are in truth not his own words at all. On the contrary, in his final statement the steward gestures towards the Foucauldian 'analytic of finitude'. Man is, Michel Foucault argues, 'a vehicle for words which exist before him':

> All these contents that his knowledge reveals to him as exterior to himself, and older than his own birth, anticipate him, overhang him with all their solidity, and traverse him as though he were merely an object of nature, a face doomed to be erased in the course of history.[72]

Manston's confession is necessarily embodied in the deathly anonymity of language. The signifier recalls the subject to a knowledge of his own finitude in a writing which, in the death-cell scene of *Desperate Remedies*, threatens any claim to self-presence of human speech.

Notes

1. J. Bayley, *An Essay on Hardy* (Cambridge: Cambridge University Press, 1978), p. 127.
2. P. de Man, *Blindness and Insight* (London: Methuen, 1983), p. 43.
3. De Man, *Blindness*, p. 44.
4. De Man, *Blindness*, p. 45.
5. De Man, *Blindness*, p. 45.
6. De Man, *Blindness*, pp. 45-46.
7. De Man, *Blindness*, p. 46.
8. De Man, *Blindness*, p. 47.
9. De Man, *Blindness*, p. 48.
10. P. de Man, *Allegories of Reading* (New Haven: Yale University Press, 1979), p. 10.
11. J. Derrida, *Of Grammatology* (trans. G.C. Spivak; Baltimore: Johns Hopkins University Press, 1976), p. 163.
12. H. Bloom, *The Anxiety of Influence* (Oxford: Oxford University Press, 1975), p. 14.
13. Bloom, *Anxiety*, p. 20.
14. Bloom, *Anxiety*, p. 21.
15. Bloom, *Anxiety*, pp. 44-45.
16. Macherey, *Literary Production*, p. 50.
17. Sigmund Freud, *The Interpretation of Dreams* (ed. A. Richards; trans. J. Strachey; Harmondsworth: Penguin Books, 1976), p. 518.
18. Prefatory Note, 1889.
19. *Roland Barthes by Roland Barthes* (trans. R. Howard; London: Macmillan, 1977), p. 143.
20. *Roland Barthes*, p. 136.

21. J. Derrida, *Glas* (Paris: Galilée, 1974), p. 146.

22. Woolf, *Collected Essays*, p. 257.

23. J. Weeks, *Sex, Politics and Society* (London: Longman, 1981), p. 116.

24. L. Irigaray, 'Sexual Difference', in T. Moi (ed.), *French Feminist Thought* (Oxford: Basil Blackwell, 1987), p. 122.

25. Thomas Hardy, *The Life and Work of Thomas Hardy* (ed. M. Millgate; London: Macmillan, 1984), pp. 23-24.

26. M. Millgate, *Thomas Hardy* (Oxford: Oxford University Press, 1985), p. 47.

27. Sigmund Freud, 'Family Romances', in *On Sexuality* (trans J. Strachey; ed A. Richards; Harmondsworth: Penguin Books, 1977), pp. 222-23.

28. L. Irigaray, cited in Jane Gallop, *Feminism and Psychoanalysis: The Daughter's Seduction* (London: Macmillan, 1982), p. 116.

29. J. Lacan, *Ecrits* (trans. A. Sheridan; London: Tavistock Publications, 1980), p. 104.

30. L. Mulvey, *Visual and Other Pleasures* (London: Macmillan, 1989), pp. 14-15.

31. Mulvey, *Pleasures*, p. 15.

32. Letter of 25 January 1920, in *The Collected Letters of Thomas Hardy*, VI (ed. R.L. Purdy and M. Millgate; London: Clarendon Press, 1987), p. 87.

33. J.F. MacCannell, *Figuring Lacan* (London: Croom Helm, 1986), pp. 7-8.

34. MacCannell, *Figuring Lacan*, p. 8.

35. MacCannell, *Figuring Lacan*, p. 8.

36. Lacan, *Ecrits*, pp. 218-19.

37. R. Williams, *The Country and the City* (London: Chatto & Windus, 1973), p. 200.

38. G. Wotton, *Thomas Hardy: Towards a Materialist Criticism* (Dublin: Gill & Macmillan, 1985), p. 52.

39. C. Bloom, *The Occult Experience and the New Criticism* (Brighton: Harvester, 1986), p. 80.

40. Bloom, *Occult Experience*, p. 81.

41. Bloom, *Occult Experience*, p. 82.

42. Bloom, *Occult Experience*, p. 84.

43. Bloom, *Occult Experience*, p. 85.

44. Bloom, *Occult Experience*, p. 84.

45. Bloom, *Occult Experience*, p. 86.

46. Bloom, *Occult Experience*, p. 87.

47. Cited in *Landscape with Figures: An Anthology of Richard Jefferies's Prose* (ed. R. Mabey; Harmondsworth: Penguin Books, 1983), p. 16.

48. Walter Benjamin, *Charles Baudelaire* (trans. H. Zohn; London: Verso, 1983), p. 43.

49. Benjamin, *Charles Baudelaire*, p. 121.

50. *Life*, p. 215.

51. Walter Benjamin, *One-Way Street and Other Writings* (trans. E. Jephcott and K. Shorter; London: Verso, 1985), p. 53.

52. Benjamin, *Charles Baudelaire*, pp. 132-33.

53. J. Rignall, 'Benjamin's *Flâneur* and the Problem of Realism', in *The Problems of Modernity: Adorno and Benjamin* (ed. A. Benjamin; London: Routledge, 1989), p. 113.

54. Rignall, 'Benjamin's *Flâneur*', p. 114.

55. Rignall, 'Benjamin's *Flâneur*', p. 114.

56. Rignall, 'Benjamin's *Flâneur*', p. 119.

57. See J. Wolff, 'The Invisible *Flâneuse*', in *The Problems of Modernity*, pp. 141-56.

58. T. Eagleton, *Walter Benjamin* (London: Verso, 1981), p. 25.

59. Eagleton, *Walter Benjamin*, p. 26.

60. Eagleton, *Walter Benjamin*, pp. 35-36.

61. Benjamin, *One-Way Street*, p. 294.

62. N. Lukacher, *Primal Scenes* (Ithaca, NY: Cornell University Press, 1986), p. 282.

63. Benjamin, *One-Way Street*, p. 314.

64. Lukacher, *Primal Scenes*, p. 283.

65. Walter Benjamin, *The Origin of German Tragic Drama* (trans. J. Osborne; London: Verso, 1985), p. 152.

66. Benjamin, *One-Way Street*, p. 314.

67. Walter Benjamin, *Illuminations* (ed. H. Arendt; trans. H. Zohn; London: Fontana, 1973), p. 98.

68. Benjamin, *Illuminations*, p. 98.

69. Benjamin, *Charles Baudelaire*, p. 134.

70. *Charles Baudelaire*, p. 100.

71. Lukacher, *Primal Scenes*, p. 286.

72. M. Foucault, *The Order of Things* (London: Tavistock Publications, 1974), p. 313.

Chapter 2

THE TRUMPET-MAJOR (1880)

On Waterloo Day, 18 June 1875, Thomas Hardy visited Chelsea
Hospital to talk to survivors of the battle sixty years before. It was one
of several such visits, and the novelist was fascinated to hear from a
veteran how the only things visible in the haze of battle were the
shining surfaces of 'bayonets, helmets, and swords'.[1] The following
year the novelist made a pilgrimage to the battlefield itself. From the
moment of his childhood discovery of a Napoleonic scrapbook com-
piled by his grandfather, a private in the Puddletown Volunteer Light
Infantry, Hardy's imagination had been fired by stories of the
Napoleonic era. Indeed, the sources of *The Trumpet-Major* and *The
Dynasts* lay far back in the stories of the invasion scare in Dorset with
which his paternal grandmother, Mary Head Hardy, had regaled the
family. The oral record of that time formed part of what the novel
calls 'the unwritten history of England' (*TM*, p. 67). Material for the
composition of the novel was assembled not only in the British
Museum but also in the houses, lanes and fields of Dorset, 'collected
from old people still living or recently deceased', as Hardy informed
the Royal Librarian in 1880.[2] In fictionalizing the scenes of war
preparation, *The Trumpet-Major* drew upon oral sources in folk
memory; it also, through the figure of Captain Hardy, stressed familial links and communal enterprise in the defence of the south coast. In
his poem 'One We Knew', dedicated to his grandmother, Hardy affec-
tionately recalled her stories:

> She told of that far-back day when they learnt astounded
>   Of the death of the King of France:
> Of the Terror, and then of Buonaparte's unbounded
>   Ambition and arrogance.
>
> Of how his threats woke warlike preparations
>   Along the southern strand,

And how each night brought tremors and trepidations
Lest morning should see him land (*CP*, p. 275).

It is this stress of immediacy and uncertainty which the novel, with the historian's perspective of hindsight, dramatizes in its impact upon a remote rural community invaded by a defending army. Trivial incidents take on a historical significance and gravity beyond the consciousness of the participants. Thus the 'cheerful, careless, unpremeditated half-hour' when the troops enjoy Miller Loveday's cherries, is to return to the memory of the participants 'when they lay wounded and weak in foreign lands' (*TM*, p. 76). The stability and continuity of rural life is both endorsed and undercut by the historical omniscience of the narrative voice, as in the evocation of the downs at the close of the military review:

> They still spread their grassy surface to the sun as on that beautiful morning not, historically speaking, so very long ago; but the King and his fifteen thousand armed men, the horses, the bands of music, the princesses, the cream-coloured teams—the gorgeous centrepiece, in short, to which the downs were but the mere mount or margin—how entirely have they all passed and gone!—lying scattered about the world as military and other dust, some at Talavera, Albuera, Salamanca, Vittoria, Toulouse, and Waterloo; some in home churchyards; and a few small handfuls in royal vaults (*TM*, p. 150).

This premonitory note is sounded with most foreboding in the carefully revised ending, when John Loveday, with his companions, departs to 'blow his trumpet till silenced for ever upon one of the bloody battle-fields of Spain' (*TM*, p. 377).

It is a note which signifies not only heroic martial deeds. There is also a sense in the novel of the invasion of ordinary lives, an unsettlement of the agricultural round, by forces of change dramatically embodied in the arrival of royalty at Budmouth. The everyday people at the centre of the action are touched by historical events, as Anne recognizes when she sees the king walking on the esplanade:

> Anne now felt herself close to and looking into the stream of recorded history, within whose banks the littlest things are great, and outside which she and the general bulk of the human race were content to live on as an unreckoned, unheeded superfluity (*TM*, p. 152).

History, Hardy was to note a few years later, 'is rather a stream than a tree',[3] and it is in the antithetical images of stream and mill that the novel makes its central binary opposition between stability and change. The scrupulous description of Overcombe Mill foregrounds the symbolic role of the mill as a workplace embodying an immemorial agrarian way of life:

> Overcombe Mill presented at one end the appearance of a hard-worked house slipping into the river, and at the other of an idle, genteel place, half-cloaked with creepers at this time of the year, and having no visible connection with flour. It had hips instead of gables, giving it a round-shouldered look, four chimneys with no smoke coming out of them, two zigzag cracks in the wall, several open windows, with a looking-glass here and there inside, showing its warped back to the passer-by; snowy dimity curtains waving in the draught; two mill doors, one above the other, the upper enabling a person to step out upon nothing at a height of ten feet from the ground; a gaping arch vomiting the river, and a lean, long-nosed fellow looking out from the mill doorway, who was the hired grinder, except when a bulging fifteen-stone man occupied the same place, namely, the miller himself (*TM*, pp. 67-68).

It is significant that both the mill, anthropomorphically described here, and Oxwell Hall are perceived in a state of 'declension'. The emphasis, in the people who 'stood to smoke and consider things', and the cats who 'slept on the clean surfaces' (*TM*, p. 68), is upon quietism and continuity. This accords with Hardy's reading of history, as revealed in a note of 1884:

> Is not the present quasi-scientific system of writing history mere charlatanism? Events and tendencies are traced as if they were rivers of voluntary activity, and courses reasoned out from the circumstances in which natures, religions, or what-not, have found themselves. But are they not in the main the outcome of *passivity*—acted upon by unconscious propensity?[4]

Rustic passivity, massively embodied in Miller Loveday, is jolted and shaken by the arrival of the military; and yet the text simultaneously urges the absorbent powers of the old way of life, as when the cavalrymen cross the threshold of the mill-house, 'the paving of which was worn into a gutter by the ebb and flow of feet that had been going on there ever since Tudor times' (*TM*, p. 81). Once snugly ensconced in the mill-house, the soldiery are enveloped by an ancient cycle which frames the urgency of the national peril, so that the swarming of the miller's bees, 'the number of his chickens, and the fatness of his pigs, were matters of infinitely greater concern' than military questions (*TM*, p. 92).

This evocation of the local and customary within the larger cycles of history is typical of the aims and concerns of a time-haunted novelist like Hardy. As Raymond Williams pointed out, the strategy of the backward glance commonly enabled the nineteenth-century novelist to recreate an illusion of a society which was harmonious and continuous:

> A valuing society, the common condition of a knowable community, belongs ideally in the past. It can be recreated there for a widely ranging moral action. But the real step that has been taken is withdrawal from any full response to an existing society.[5]

The pressures and contradictions of contemporary rural society which inform and energize Hardy's most potent texts in their polyphonic richness are notably absent from *The Trumpet-Major*. Withdrawal into a warlike past paradoxically produces a text of anodyne smoothness. Yet contradictions working against the collusion in an agrarian myth of community are discernible in the texture of the prose at the very point where Hardy evokes the rustic symbolism of the mill. The opening of the second chapter unconsciously reveals, in its tracing of the lineage of the miller, the economic reality beneath the myth:

> Miller Loveday was the representative of an ancient family of corn-grinders whose history is lost in the mists of antiquity. His ancestral line was contemporaneous with that of De Ros, Howard, and De La Zouche; but, owing to some trifling deficiency in the possessions of the house of Loveday, the individual names and intermarriages of its members were not recorded during the Middle Ages, and thus their private lives in any given century were uncertain. But it was known that the family had formed matrimonial alliances with farmers not so very small, and once with a gentleman-tanner, who had for many years purchased after their death the horses of the most aristocratic persons in the county—fiery steeds that earlier in their career had been valued at many hundred guineas (*TM*, p. 67).

As George Wotton has observed, this passage is one of those 'nodal points' in Hardy's writing, where 'the unity of allusion to recorded history' and 'the imaginary history of Wessex' coalesce to reveal 'the "real" history of England'. Presence in the historical record, Wotton argues, 'depends on land *ownership*':

> The *apparent* history of England is thus nothing more than the record of the private lives of the large owners of property, a record which conceals the *real* but unwritten history of the Lovedays and the class they represent.[6]

This is not to belittle Hardy's aims in writing *The Trumpet-Major*, though the comparison with another mill-owning family, the Tullivers in *The Mill on the Floss*, may suggest how modest its achievement is in the recreation of an 'unwritten history' of the people. Yet the project of *The Trumpet-Major*, in connecting the Garlands, Lovedays and Derrimans with historical forces, could scarcely be of greater significance. Georg Lukács, in analysing the genesis of the historical novel, observed that it was the French Revolution, and the rise and fall of Napoleon, 'which for the first time made history a *mass experience*, and moreover on a European scale'.[7] In effecting 'an extraordinary broadening of horizons', Lukács suggested, the Napoleonic wars brought into being 'the concrete possibilities for men to comprehend their own experience as something historically conditioned, for them to see in history something which deeply affects their daily lives and immediately concerns them'.[8] This is precisely the aim of *The Trumpet-Major*, one of that series of works inhabited, as Hardy wrote in his General Preface of 1912, by 'beings in whose hearts and minds that which is apparently local' is 'really universal'.

But to invoke Lukács is implicitly to call up memories of *War and Peace* and thus to expose with pitiless clarity the narrow range of Hardy's achievement here. In its painstaking documentation, *The Trumpet-Major* hovers on the verge of what Lukács characterized as 'a deadening preponderance of antiquarianism'[9] in the historical novel of the later nineteenth century. Certainly the action of the novel does little to endorse Lukács's belief that history is a gradual realization of the full potential of man. The comparison with *War and Peace* is invidious but instructive. What Hazlitt said of Scott might also refer to Hardy's conscientious fact-gathering for the composition of *The Trumpet-Major*: 'Our historical novelist firmly thinks that nothing *is* but what *has been*'.[10]

Nevertheless, though the story was evidently conceived at low pressure, the writer's imagination was fired by the events and traces of the Napoleonic period in Wessex—the door riddled with bullet holes, the hut of the beacon-watchers, the decaying pikes, and the ridges of the encampment to which he refers in the Preface—and by that less tangible record available to the novelist through 'oral relation' (*TM*, p. 58). The difficulty in such writing, as the Preface acknowledges, is 'to construct a coherent narrative of past times' out of such 'fragmentary information' (*TM*, p. 57). Much of the interest of *The Trumpet-Major* derives from Hardy's shaping of these miscellaneous materials into a narrative for his magazine audience.

In his examination of the processes of the nineteenth-century historical imagination, *Metahistory*, Hayden White offers some illuminating
comments upon the relations of fictional narrative to historical source
material. White designates chronicle and story as 'primitive elements'
in the historical account. The arrangement of material entailed by a
narrative such as Hardy's represents a 'process of selection and
arrangement of data from the *unprocessed historical record* in the
interest of rendering that record more comprehensible to an *audience*
of a particular kind'.[11] Story is structured, White argues, in terms of
inaugural, transitional and terminating motifs, and historical studies
thus trace 'the sequence of events that lead from inaugurations to
(provisional) terminations of social and cultural processes'.[12] A novel
like *The Trumpet-Major* consists of a conjunction of real and
imagined events arranged in some kind of hierarchy of significance,
and its tone and structure conform to White's definition of comedy. In
comedy, he argues, 'hope is held out for the temporary triumph of
man over his world by the prospect of occasional *reconciliations* of
the forces at play', and these reconciliations are 'symbolised in the
festive occasions' which terminate 'dramatic accounts of change and
transformation'.[13] Thus the marriages of Miller Loveday and Mrs
Garland and Festus and Matilda, the victory of Trafalgar, the final
coming together of Anne and Bob, and Anne's inheritance of the
miser's wealth and property effectively limit and terminate the
destabilizing effects of the invasion threat. At the same time, White
insists upon the way comedy allows for the emergence of 'new forces
or conditions out of processes that appear at a glance to be changeless
in their essence'.[14] Beneath the placid surface of Wessex life there is
radical unsettlement, a dynamic of change symbolized by the arrival
of the soldiery and royalty, but also signalled by the status changes
suffered or enjoyed by the protagonists. Thus Mrs Garland falls
socially by her second marriage, whilst the miller paradoxically gains
respectability; Anne, having fallen through her mother's alliance and
her own connection with Bob, rises through her unexpected inheritance to a position of wealth and power; Matilda escapes from the low
status and nomadic life of the actress through her liaison with Festus,
whilst the latter falls through the demise of his large expectations.
Wessex is shot through with change, just as Budmouth is transformed
from its status as a modest resort by the arrival of the royal family.

As White sees it, historical explanation may be categorized in a variety of paradigms, and his definition of the 'organicist' model is of some relevance to *The Trumpet-Major*. An organicist reading of history arises out of a 'desire to see individual entities as components or processes which aggregate into wholes that are greater than, or qualitatively different from, the sum of their parts'. Thus the Dorset of the Napoleonic era may be characterized as an 'integrated entity whose importance is greater than that of any individual entities analysed or described in the course of the narrative'.[15]

Narrative implies continuity, and continuity implies memory. As a novel founded in familial and communal memories of a great crisis, *The Trumpet-Major* celebrates the potency of memory and expresses that potency in its idyllic tone of voice. Yet communal memory and the immediacy of oral transmission appear to be curiously threatened in the novel. There is a remarkable degree of emphasis here upon the written record which is insidiously replacing speech. Anne's readings of the newspaper to Uncle Benjy, and the reliance upon letters and newspapers at the mill as guarantors of truth and reality, attest to a subtle shift in this society from speech to writing, from presence to absence, plenitude to emptiness. Language here, as elsewhere in the Wessex novels, is losing its dialectal vitality and substance as it becomes increasingly embalmed in the formality of script. It is no accident that the central relationships for Anne Garland, those with John and Bob Loveday, are marked by prolonged periods of absence and silence, or that the overwhelming presence in the novel is that of the absent Napoleon. A movement in the community from speech to writing prefigures an alienation of relationship which Hardy will finally dissect in the highly literary text of *Jude the Obscure*. The easygoing virtues of *The Trumpet-Major* as a novel which mutedly celebrates love, patriotism and traditional life conceal underlying dissonances which lurk beneath the text.

History, Foucault has written, 'is that which transforms *documents* into *monuments*'.[16] Hardy, in his careful preparation for the novel, consciously sought such a transformation. Covertly, the text also seeks to aggrandize the Hardys and their place in Dorset history by claiming kinship with Captain Hardy, whose physical monument dominated the south-west of the county. The documents consulted at the British Museum provided foundations for the novelist's sly erection of his own familial monument, a monument built out of the primacy of writing over an older oral culture whose disappearance it records. Beneath the smoothly homogeneous discourse of *The Trumpet-Major* may be discerned other discourses: the novel operates like history in transforming and suppressing its own sources. As Foucault remarks, history can 'lend speech to those traces which, in themselves, are often not verbal, or which say in silence something other than what they actually say'.[17] The writer's imagination, exercising mastery over the historical material, utilizes that material to assert and validate its own existence. The narrative background of *The Trumpet-Major* fascinates its creator as part of his own prehistory. Foucault has argued that the writing of history is 'the indispensable correlative of the founding function of the subject'.[18] The mastery evinced by the narrative voice in the novel, with its grasp of wide historical movements, its fore-knowledge of the course of individual lives, and its sure command of uncertainties, endorses Foucault's claim as to the underlying project of the historical writer, who seeks

> the guarantee that everything that has eluded him may be restored to him; the certainty that time will disperse nothing without restoring it in a reconstituted unity; the promise that one day the subject—in the form of historical consciousness—will once again be able to appropriate. . . all those things that are kept at a distance by difference, and find in them what might be called his abode.[19]

The relationship of a fictional narrative like *The Trumpet-Major* to its historical sources is a complex matter of continuous reinterpretation and creative misprision.

In the midst of history, yet marginal to it, the novelist places his love story. But, dwarfed and drained of significance by the Napoleonic manoeuvres around them, the protagonists of *The Trumpet-Major* are pallid and uninvolved, as if the novelist's eye is fascinatedly held upon the 'shining surfaces' observed by the veteran of Waterloo. As characters the people are all surface. The ill-fated passions of previous novels have here dwindled into timidity and self-interest, the riddling metaphoric richness of earlier texts thinned out to produce a carefully controlled and processed story. Hardy turns the plot upon his favourite motif of a woman pursued by a number of men, but the resultant drama of mismatching is tepid and manufac-tured, the heroine constrained to exist silently in a world dominated and preserved by the male implements of sword and pen. Anne Garland is an absent centre, and her suitors exert little power over heroine or reader. The trumpet-major himself functions through repression and self-abnegation to such a degree that the heroism upon which the narrator insists begins to feel psychotic. The extrovert Bob

Loveday, by contrast, vacillates between a range of unsuitable partners in an arbitrary manner suggested by exigencies of plot rather
than character. The third suitor, Festus Derriman, never rises above
his origins as *miles gloriosus*, and his fate is wholly predictable. The
textual effect of these machinations is a curious emptiness of characterization, as if the narrator has hidden the key to the characters'
actions as stealthily as the old miser hides his guineas.

Hardy's deepest imaginative investment goes into the conjuring up
of the invasion scare, but the novel does bear traces of characteristic
effects and devices in its handling of relationships. The characters of
The Trumpet-Major are at once transparently simple and bafflingly
opaque, and the situations into which they are thrown by the narrative
gain in resonance through the prevalent notion of perception as the
generating principle of relationship. Anne Garland, significantly
deprived of a protective father and provided with a girlishly irre-
sponsible mother, is, in the originating moment of the novel, sitting at
a window of the mill-house working at a hearth-rug. Looking out
from the open casement towards the mill-pond and the bare downland
beyond, the heroine is surprised by the sudden arrival of two cavalry
soldiers, followed by 'a whole column of cavalry in marching order'
(*TM*, p. 62), arriving, as soon becomes clear, to camp on the downs.
This crucial scenario, with the isolated heroine looking outwards from
her casement upon the soldiery beyond, will be repeated later in her
observation of the 'panoramic procession' of the troops wheeling off
on parade (*TM*, p. 76). It is a moment which inscribes the status and
role of the heroine as a girl deprived of 'thriving male relatives' (*TM*,
p. 113), simultaneously drawn towards, and withdrawing 'prim and
stiff' (*TM*, p. 77) from, the event outside. Anne Garland, like other
Hardy heroines, conforms to a kind of Lady of Shalott syndrome. The
soldiers attract the passive female observer through colourful display,
a change at the manuscript stage emphasizing the 'burnished chains,
buckles, and plates' which 'shone like little looking-glasses', accoutrements reflecting 'the sun through the haze' (as Hardy visualized
Waterloo), 'in faint flashes, stars, and streaks of light' (*TM*, pp. 62-
63). Tennyson's heroine, similarly circumstanced, abandons her
weaving to observe the glinting surfaces of Sir Lancelot's equipage:

> All in the blue unclouded weather
> Thick-jewell'd shone the saddle-leather,
> The helmet and the helmet-feather

Burn'd like one burning flame together,
As he rode down to Camelot.

Analysis of the recurrent Lady of Shalott situation in Victorian fiction has identified a number of motifs associated with Anne Garland's posture at the opening of the novel. It is suggested that the heroine in this situation is commonly imprisoned 'in the midst of an expansive landscape that sustains a working community'.[20] It is a state of entrapment which may be characterized as one of 'self-enclosed gentility', imposed as much 'by the values ascribed' to the heroine as 'by the deprivations of a diminished life'.[21] There is a dramatic division, therefore, between the glamorized exterior world of male energy and the withdrawn inner space of an onlooking female passivity. The war-like sphere of masculine endeavour (parodied and thus endorsed by Festus Derriman) allows for the changefulness and instability emblematized in the weathercock which displays the figure of a soldier (John Loveday) transformed into the figure of a sailor (Bob Loveday). Indeed, the 'variable currents in the wind' (*TM*, p. 68) aptly characterize the motivation both of 'that weathercock, Master Bob' (*TM*, p. 343), and of the comically volcanic Festus. In the world of *The Trumpet-Major*, 'greedy carnivorous man' (*TM*, p. 69) predominates, and this domination, desire and mastery are expressed through sight.

Hardy once observed that 'Love lives on propinquity, but dies of contact',[22] and the sexual chess-games of *The Trumpet-Major* are predicated upon this notion. J. Hillis Miller has drawn attention to the way, in Hardy, that the 'direct encounter, eye to eye in open reciprocity, is often only the final stage before sexual possession in a drama of looks which begins with some form of spying or the look unreturned'.[23] The plot turns upon misalliances founded in perception. As Hillis Miller remarks, 'Once the situation of desire has been established, often a tangled one involving a criss-cross of mismatching loves, the form of each novel is determined by the development of these loves'.[24] Desire is mediated through the glance, and the pattern of courtship in Hardy is often of the kind of approach and withdrawal which typifies Bob's behaviour.

Looking, seeing and being seen, and spying predominate as modes of relationship in *The Trumpet-Major*. Anne, protected by her casement, is alarmed to see Festus Derriman standing below in the mill-pond. Knocking on her lattice with his whip, he 'looked up, and their eyes met' (*TM*, p. 118). He then strikes another blow against her window. The impatient suggestion of attempted penetration here is characteristic and is one which the story unconsciously mobilizes later. The scene is further complicated in its 'conjunction of incidents' by John Loveday's astounded sighting of Festus beneath Anne's window. Such erotic conjunctions have been prepared in the previous scene when Anne, reading the newspaper to Squire Derriman, becomes conscious of 'the bothering yeoman's eyes. . . creeping over her shoulders, up to her head, and across her arms and hands' (*TM*, p. 114). Later in the novel the trumpet-major himself is voyeuristically to watch in the darkness as Anne enters her bedroom and closes her casement (*TM*, p. 211). The final turn of events is engineered through a reversal in which the female secretly watches the 'pretty spectacle' of Bob Loveday ludicrously parading in full uniform in the garden (*TM*, p. 362), a scene whose sexual implications feebly echo Troy's sword-play before Bathsheba. Bob, indeed, as able-bodied seaman comes to feel entrapped into this dalliance: the '"pleasure of sighting that young girl forty times a day, and letting her sight me"', he feels, is little compensation for his absence from the male world of ships and action (*TM*, p. 305). '"Womankind has hampered me"', he explains to Captain Hardy (*TM*, p. 312), an explanation which both captain and novel endorse.

Elsewhere, images of sight also serve to dramatize the enforced passivity of the hidden female, as when Anne is constrained to watch the village flirtations from her window (*TM*, p. 129). Even the dynamic Matilda Johnson is secretly observed by the trumpet-major, 'standing before the looking-glass, apparently lost in thought' (*TM*, p. 189), her witty self-preservation evaporating at the news of his knowledge of her compromised past. The sense of complication, of the acquisition of secret power and knowledge, is communicated in various scenes of spying, or in a network of reciprocal glances. John Loveday, having boxed Festus's ears to avenge the insult to Anne, is then humiliatingly forced to hide in the granary while, below, Bob and Anne exchange endearments (*TM*, p. 274). Later, Anne will watch the feints and counterfeits of Festus and Uncle Benjy through a knot-hole in the floor of the mill-house (*TM*, p. 372). But the most complex web of erotic contingency is traced in the theatre scene. Here, Bob and Anne, believing John to be in love with an actress, watch his face for signs of emotion. A 'deadlock of awkward suspense' occurs when Matilda Johnson appears on stage and sights both her former fiancé and the trumpet-major in the audience (*TM*,

p. 286). The scene is handled lightly for its comic potential, but it serves to concentrate the predominance of sight as the defining metaphor for sexuality, passivity and domination in *The Trumpet-Major*.

The paradoxical construction of meanings in the novel through this shifting drama of eye, glance and gaze may be explicated by the Lacanian theory of the 'scopic drive'. Lacan bases his thesis about the construction of the subject in desire upon the act of seeing. Through the gaze, which Freud argued was ultimately derived from touch, the subject defines and establishes him or herself in a function of desire. The gaze is the 'underside of consciousness',[25] and in the gaze of the male (John Loveday, Bob Loveday, Festus Derriman) through Anne Garland's casement window, *The Trumpet-Major* metaphorically presents a phallic penetration. Lacan argues that 'it is in so far as all human desire is based on castration that the eye assumes its virulent, aggressive function'.[26] The gaze is 'symbolic of what we find on the horizon, as the thrust of our experience, namely, the lack that constitutes castration anxiety'.[27] The unconscious flow of desire in looking causes what Lacan terms a *méconnaissance* or mistaken seeing in the perceiving subject, since every act of visualization is founded in a conflictual play of repression of the unconscious, a dialectic of desire and lack, presence and absence. The kind of display in which the uniformed Bob Loveday indulges in the garden below Anne's window acts out the way the exhibitionist seeks through his behaviour for the confirmation of his desire in the imagined desire of the other. As Lacan phrases it,

> In the case of display, usually on the part of the male animal, or in the case of grimacing swelling by which the animal enters the play of combat in the form of intimidation, the being gives of itself, or receives from the other, something that is like a mask, a double, an envelope, a thrown-off skin, thrown off in order to cover the frame of a shield.[28]

This 'combat in the form of intimidation' which Lacan identifies with the reproductive drive is aptly characteristic of the enlisted Bob Loveday, or of Festus Derriman, archetypal *miles gloriosus*. Similarly, the voyeurism which marks this and other Hardy novels also formulates desire as looking. Lacan claims that 'When, in love, I solicit a look, what is profoundly unsatisfying and always missing is that—*You never look at me from the place from which I see you*'.[29] The lover thus narcissistically projects the desire of the other as completion of his own incompleteness. Reality, in Lacan as in Hardy, does not correspond to wish. In the economy of Hardy's writing the female often figures as the object of a look which is either voyeuristic or fetishistic, both forms, in a Lacanian sense, responding to a threat of castration always evoked in the male by the female body. Voyeurism, the mode which predominates in *The Trumpet-Major*, is associated with the aggression of warfare. The act of narration itself seems to privilege the male gaze and to fetishize the female in its representation of male and female subjects. In the persuasive nuances of the narrative voice the reader colludes with this representation. Sexual difference is indissolubly linked in Hardy to representational images of the body; in this fiction sexual difference is both immutably fixed and troublingly excessive to both author and reader. Absence and difference are at the heart of such transactions, just as the meaning of the plot of *The Trumpet-Major* is founded in the absence of lover or invader. Feminist responses to Lacan, stressing the way in which the male eye objectifies and masters what it sees, are also germane to the patriarchal world of *The Trumpet-Major*. The female looking out on to the world as subject at the opening is rapidly transformed through plot into an object of the excited male gaze. The female body, set in a carefully eroticized topography of (female) mill-pond and (male) downland, is transmuted into a fetish which is stared at voyeuristically by the controlling male with his weaponry.

The female is thus equated with passivity and lack, an equation which the narrative endorses in the erased presence of Anne as heroine. By positing a series of binary oppositions—male/female, war/peace, active/passive—the novel is able to define the female as a negative opposite to the male, a figure characterized by acquiescence and invisibility. In Matilda Johnson, the novel displaces, focuses and revives Anne Garland's censored sexuality with revealing ambiguity. Matilda is a free-wheeling opportunist whose role-playing wit and energy threaten male power and the patriarchal values of the plot. She acts as the silent Anne's *alter ego*, but is placed judgmentally through the stern moralism of John Loveday and casually paired off with Festus Derriman. Having disposed of the threat posed by Matilda's openly declared sexuality and freedom, the brothers collude over the disposal of Anne, passing the girl between them like a parcel of goods. As D.H. Lawrence remarked, the women Hardy's plots approve 'are not Female in any real sense', but are rather 'passive subjects to the male', while 'all exceptional or strong individual traits he holds up as weaknesses or wicked faults'.[30]

The Trumpet-Major is a text marked by a timidity and censorship produced jointly by the low pressure of the writer's imagination and the proprieties of magazine publication. The contingency of history spells death to the erotic. But at one critical juncture this textual self-effacement collapses to allow a dissonant scene which erupts disturbingly into the rural idyll. Festus Derriman's 'uncontrollable affection' (*TM*, p. 226) is typically blocked by the heroine, as when she converses with him from behind the hedge (*TM*, p. 203). But this blocking stratagem fails her at the crisis. The scene where, locked in the deserted house, the heroine is threatened by the enraged Festus Derriman takes the form of a covert rape scene which enacts the secret desires of the text in its bafflement with the passivity of its heroine. Festus is 'brimful of suppressed passion' (*TM*, p. 265), a passion inflamed by the docility of his quarry. The fascinated but inconclusive scrutinies of earlier window scenes give way to a direct confrontation which unbalances the neutral narrative voice and destroys the equilibrium achieved elsewhere through the seeping away of energy and passion from the text. Anne's characteristic reaction of barricading herself from the proffered transaction, and her vacillation about accepting Festus's attentions, serve only to arouse and inflame. Derriman seeks to penetrate the inner space of the house in order to enact those desires which the book as a whole muffles and distorts. What is repressed in the narrative returns here with a vengeance. In Derriman's final desperate act the text, radically unaware of its own gesture, unites wished-for phallic penetration with unconsciously feared castration:

> peeping over the window-sill, she saw her tormentor drive his sword between the joints of the shutters, in an attempt to rip them open. The sword snapped off in his hand. With an imprecation he pulled out the piece, and returned the two halves to the scabbard (*TM*, p. 264).

It is a revealing moment, the secret signification of the pervasive imagery of weapons and war momentarily leaping out of hiding in the text's unavowed fascination with violence. The bragging volunteer seeks to penetrate the heroine just as the absently threatening figure of the 'Corsican Ogre' seeks, through his armies, to penetrate the English defences. The construction, in *The Trumpet-Major*, of a male/female binary opposition which informs both historical and romantic plots and the covert alliance in bellicose masculinist ardour of Festus Derriman and the Loveday brothers with the invading emperor, is illuminated by a passage in Virginia Woolf's *A Room of One's Own*. Women, Woolf argues, 'have served all these centuries as looking-glasses' with the power of 'reflecting the figure of man at twice its natural size'. Without this power, the 'glories' of war would be unknown:

> Supermen and Fingers of Destiny would never have existed. The Tsar and the Kaiser would never have worn crowns or lost them. Whatever may be their use in civilised societies, mirrors are essential to all violent and heroic action. That is why Napoleon and Mussolini both insist so emphatically upon the inferiority of women, for if they were not inferior, they would cease to enlarge.

The looking-glass vision is of 'supreme importance because it charges the vitality' and 'stimulates the nervous system' of the male. If the woman begins to tell the truth, Woolf suggests, 'the figure in the looking-glass shrinks'; 'his fitness for life is diminished'.[31] Woolf's case may be glossed by reference to Toril Moi's exposition of the way Freud is subjected to re-reading in French feminism. Luce Irigaray, Moi suggests, concludes that 'woman is outside representation', she is the 'negative required by the male subject's "specularisation"'. The notion of specularization, which is so crucial to the plot of *The Trumpet-Major*, is founded, Moi argues, upon 'a basic assumption underlying all Western philosophical discourse: the necessity of postulating a subject that is capable of *reflecting* on its own being'; philosophical (male) discourse is thus fundamentally narcissistic:

> Disguised as reflections on the general condition of man's Being, the philosopher's thinking depends for its effect on its specularity (its self-reflexivity); that which exceeds this reflective circularity is that which is *unthinkable*. It is this kind of specul(aris)ation Irigaray has in mind when she argues that Western philosophical discourse is incapable of representing femininity/woman other than as the negative of its *own* reflection.

Located within the Freudian thesis of penis envy, and the related stress upon the will to mastery of the male gaze, Irigaray demonstrates how woman is reduced to the function of 'a mirror'. Indeed, both Anne Garland and Matilda Johnson fulfil, in Hardy's military novel, the role predicated for woman in Moi's summing up:

> Caught in the specular logic of patriarchy, woman can choose either to remain silent, producing incomprehensible babble (any utterance that falls

outside the logic of the same will by definition be incomprehensible to the
male master discourse), or to *enact* the specular representation of herself
as a lesser male.[32]

Anne escapes from Derriman's clutches, as plot and readership
demand, and Hardy disentangles the love imbroglio with a burst of
'patriotic cheerfulness' (*TM*, p. 313). With the introduction of
Captain Hardy, and Bob's subsequent departure on board the *Victory*,
Hardy invokes national myth as plot resolution, just as Tennyson had
done in *Maud*. From the nicely observed realities of mill life, the
novel turns towards a world of naval derring-do owing little to historical reality. *The Trumpet-Major* feeds upon and sustains a potently
shared communal myth to fake the energy and passion it so patently
lacks. A glance at naval history confirms the gap between a jointly
produced and consumed national myth and the reality of naval service.
The Draconian discipline enforced through flogging at the yard-arm,
low wages, lack of shore leave, poor victuals and ill health are well
attested. It was these and other contributory factors which led to the
mutinies at Spithead and the Nore in 1797, a few years prior to the
action of the novel. Seen in this context, Bob Loveday's exploits on
board the *Victory* and later ships take on the aura of a magazine story
for boys. The text similarly averts its eyes from the evidence in its
treatment of the sailors' sexual life. Bob excuses his roving eye thus:
' "When you come ashore after having been shut up in a ship for
eighteen months, women-folk seem so new and nice that you can't
help liking them, one and all in a body" '(*TM*, p. 196). This slides
disingenuously over the realities of the situation. When a ship docked
after a lengthy voyage it was common practice for it to be met by
boat-loads of prostitutes, as the 1822 'Statement of Certain Immoral
Practices in H.M. Ships' reveals: 'Let those who have never seen a
ship of war picture to themselves a very large low room. . . with five
hundred men and probably three or four hundred women of the vilest
description shut up in it, and giving way to every excess of debauch-
ery that the grossest passions of human nature can lead them to'.[33] The
cultivation of the myth of naval glory serves to create an imaginary
unified national history in the manufacture of which the text exercises
a considerable degree of censorship.

The keynote of *The Trumpet-Major* is absence: Anne's dead father,
Squire Derriman's fortune, Bob Loveday, the trumpet-major, all are
made significant through absence. Over the entire narrative broods the
absent Napoleon, expected at every moment, like Godot, but destined

never to appear. Hardy's art thrives upon postponement, bafflement, absence, to the extent that the principle of deferral becomes the structural law of the novel; deferral of military action ramifies into deferral of erotic action, and both embody a society and a text remarkably addicted to deferral of meaning. History, in the novelist's philosophical scheme, was driven forward by the Immanent Will. Yet the salient point about this brooding Will, as Hillis Miller has recognized, is its very immanence:

> It is visible only at a distance from itself, in the signs or traces of it, for example in Hardy's writings. Its coming to consciousness exists only within the images of his work. Its actual coming to consciousness is always deferred. The Will is the principle of distance, its writing always signs of itself, not its real self.[34]

The Trumpet-Major, in its repression of conflict and contradiction and its determined effacement of the female, is dangerously close to a Barthesian 'prattling text'[35] which appears impervious to interpretation. Its undeniable strengths and beauties derive from its intimate relationship with a felt and recorded historical context. The novel grew almost somnambulistically out of tap-roots deep in Wessex folk consciousness and family memory. In this story, with its curiously hypnotic blend of warlike activity and erotic passivity, Hardy mobilizes the past in service of his own myth. The narrator fascinatedly controls, and is controlled by, his story, so that the final sense the reader is left with is of a history which writes (and reads) itself.

Notes

1. *Life*, p. 109.
2. Letter of 3 December 1880, in *The Collected Letters of Thomas Hardy*, I (ed. R.L. Purdy and M. Millgate; Oxford: Clarendon Press, 1978), p. 83.
3. *Life*, p. 179.
4. *Life*, p. 175.
5. Williams, *The Country and the City*, p. 180.
6. Wotton, *Thomas Hardy*, p. 47.
7. G. Lukács, *The Historical Novel* (Harmondsworth: Penguin Books, 1969), p. 20.
8. Lukács, *The Historical Novel*, pp. 21-22.
9. Lukács, *The Historical Novel*, p. 294.
10. William Hazlitt, *The Spirit of the Age* (ed. E.D. Mackerness; London: Collins, 1969), p. 97.

11. H. White, *Metahistory* (Baltimore: Johns Hopkins University Press, 1973), p. 5.

12. White, *Metahistory*, p. 6.

13. White, *Metahistory*, p. 9.

14. White, *Metahistory*, p. 11.

15. White, *Metahistory*, p. 15.

16. M. Foucault, *The Archaeology of Knowledge* (trans. A. Sheridan Smith; London: Tavistock Publications, 1974), p. 7.

17. Foucault, *Archaeology*, p. 7.

18. Foucault, *Archaeology*, p. 12.

19. Foucault, *Archaeology*, p. 12.

20. J. Gribble, *The Lady of Shalott in the Victorian Novel* (London: Macmillan, 1983), p. 2.

21. Gribble, *Lady of Shalott*, p. 12.

22. *Life*, p. 230.

23. J. Hillis Miller, *Thomas Hardy: Distance and Desire* (Cambridge, MA: Harvard University Press, 1970), p. 120.

24. Hillis Miller, *Thomas Hardy*, pp. 146-47.

25. J. Lacan, *The Four Fundamental Concepts of Psychoanalysis* (trans. A. Sheridan; Harmondsworth: Penguin Books, 1986), p. 83.

26. Lacan, *Fundamental Concepts*, p. 118.

27. Lacan, *Fundamental Concepts*, pp. 72-73.

28. Lacan, *Fundamental Concepts*, p. 107.

29. Lacan, *Fundamental Concepts*, p. 103.

30. D.H. Lawrence, *Study of Thomas Hardy and Other Essays* (ed. B. Steele; Cambridge: Cambridge University Press, 1985), pp. 47, 95.

31. Virginia Woolf, *A Room of One's Own* (Harmondsworth: Penguin Books, 1963), pp. 37-38.

32. T. Moi, *Sexual/Textual Politics* (London: Methuen, 1985), pp. 132-35.

33. Cited in C. Lloyd, *The British Seaman* (London: Paladin, 1970), p. 225.

34. Hillis Miller, *Thomas Hardy*, p. 268.

35. R. Barthes, *The Pleasure of the Text* (trans. R. Miller; New York: Noonday Press, 1975), p. 5.

Chapter 3

OUR EXPLOITS AT WEST POLEY (1883)

The strangeness of Hardy's story for children, *Our Exploits at West Poley*, begins with its publishing history. The tale was written in the summer of 1883, before Hardy started work on *The Mayor of Casterbridge*, and was designed for an American magazine, the *Youth's Companion*. Although the story was announced in the magazine as forthcoming in 1884, despite some revision by the author it was never published there, and Hardy heard nothing further about it. Daniel Ford, editor of the *Youth's Companion*, eventually gave the manuscript to his son-in-law, who published it in a journal 'Devoted to the Interests of the American Housewife', *The Household*. In this unlikely context *Our Exploits at West Poley* was published in six monthly instalments from November 1892 to April 1893.[1] The manuscript was thus stored away for years in a filing cabinet at the offices of the *Youth's Companion*, hidden from the view of both author and public, only to appear belatedly in a somewhat inappropriate journal.

The narrator, looking back to his boyhood, recalls a visit he made at the age of thirteen to his Aunt Draycot and her son Steve, who were living in the Mendips. Mrs Draycot's husband is dead, but Leonard, the storyteller, is dominated from the outset by his more vigorous cousin:

> He was two or three years my senior, tall, lithe, ruddy, and somewhat masterful withal. There was that force about him which was less suggestive of intellectual power than (as Carlyle said of Cromwell) 'Doughtiness—the courage and faculty to do' (*OE*, p. 2).

When Leonard expresses his disappointment about the lack of grand scenery in the Mendips, Steve determines that they will explore the caves beneath the surface. The preparations for the expedition include, significantly in this tale of pubertal adventure, a number of candle-ends, and also 'a bit of board perforated with holes, into which the candles would fit' (*OE*, p. 4). The cave which they enter is 'screened by bushes' and has been 'the haunt of many boys', though 'little examined by tourists and men of science' (*OE*, p. 5). Steve boasts that this inner space is his 'home', and proceeds to lead his cousin through an archway:

> The arch gave access to a narrow tunnel or gallery, sloping downwards, and presently terminating in another cave, the floor of which spread out into a beautiful level of sand and shingle, interspersed with pieces of rock. Across the middle of this subterranean shore, as it might have been called, flowed a pellucid stream (*OE*, pp. 6-7).

Beyond the stream they discover 'a delightful recess' in the crystallized stonework, 'like the apse of a Gothic church' (*OE*, p. 7). In order to get to this 'beautiful, glistening niche' (*OE*, p. 8), the boys dig out and divert the stream. Having done so, they delight in the 'natural ornaments of the niche':

> These covered the greater part of the sides and roof; they were flesh-coloured, and assumed the form of pills, lace, coats of mail; in many places they quaintly resembled the skin of geese after plucking, and in others the wattles of turkeys. All were decorated with water crystals (*OE*, p. 10).

As the boys return to the village, their reverie is interrupted by the vigorous complaints of the villagers, led by the miller. The stream which runs through the village and turns the mill-wheel has suddenly dried up. Ignoring the counsel of the Man who had Failed, a kind of village philosopher, the miller now sees ruin staring him in the face, and the boys recognize their own culpability. They hasten to turn the stream back into its original course:

> At once we walked into the village street with an air of unconcern. The miller's face was creased with wrinkles of satisfaction: the countenance of the blacksmith, shoemaker, grocer, and dairyman were perceptibly brighter (*OE*, p. 17).

However, their new embankment proves weak, and walking over the hills to the neighbouring village of East Poley, they find great merrymaking at the sudden appearance of a new river. On returning to West Poley the boys rescue their luckless friend Job from the clutches of the irascible miller, and conclude that the diversion of the river has done more good than harm.

Employing Job to divert the stream at an agreed time, Leonard and

Steve decide to appear in East Poley in the guise of magicians with power over the flow of the new river, However, seeing a poor widow whose garden has been flooded, they realize their action is fraught with ambiguities. On returning to the cave, Job reveals that he has diverted the water into a third channel, so as to avoid starting the mill-wheel again. The boys work to block up the other two routes, not realizing that the water-level in the cave is now rising:

> Instead of pouring down out of sight, as it had been doing when we last looked, the stream was choked by a rising pool into which it boiled, showing at a glance that what we had innocently believed to be another outlet for the stream was only a third blind passage or cul-de-sac (*OE*, pp. 37-38).

It occurs to them that the two alternative passages are now impossible to free; both exits 'had been funnel-shaped cavities, narrowing down to mere fissures at the bottom' (*OE*, p. 38). Job and Steve therefore strip off 'all but their drawers' (*OE*, p. 39), and dive into the rising water to try to remove the blockages, whilst Leonard holds the candle. But their efforts are to no avail. Unbeknown to the boys, there is a shaft from above ground, and after some comic business with the miller they are finally rescued, and the stream resumes its original course. Steve suffers a fever, and reveals the secret of the cave to an assembly of villagers. Soon his revelations are betrayed to the rival men of East Poley, and on climbing up the slope to the hole above Nick's Pocket, 'a hole that probably no human being had passed through before' (*OE*, p. 67), the West Poley villagers glimpse their rivals working to divert the stream once more to their own benefit. Raids and counter-raids ensue, until Steve determines to end this rivalry by a desperate venture:

> Before I could reply, we were startled by a jet of smoke, like that from the muzzle of a gun, bursting from the mouth of Nick's Pocket; and this was immediately followed by a deadened rumble like thunder underground. In another moment a duplicate of the noise reached our ears from over the hill, in the precise direction of Grim Billy (*OE*, p. 75).

The effect of the explosion is irrevocable: 'The whole superimposed mountain, as it seemed, had quietly settled down upon the hollow places beneath it, closing like a pair of bellows, and barring all human entrance' (*OE*, p. 76). The Man who had Failed does not fail to expound the moral: '"Your courage is praiseworthy, but you see the risks that are incurred when people go out of their way to meddle

with what they don't understand"' (*OE*, p. 78). Leonard goes on to
conclude that this message has been absorbed, since Steve Draycot 'is
now the largest gentleman-farmer of those parts, remarkable for his
avoidance of anything like speculative exploits' (*OE*, p. 78).

Our Exploits at West Poley, in its direct clarity of character and
event, counts as one of Hardy's least decipherable texts. The adoption
of the naive adolescent voice and the linear narrative structure serve
to lull and bemuse the reader. In fact, Hardy's innocent narrative possesses all the crucial features of the Barthesian text of pleasure. The
more a story is told, Barthes argues, 'in a proper, well-spoken,
straightforward way, in an even tone, the easier it is to reverse it, to
blacken it, to read it inside out'.[2] That the story conceals some kinds
of biographical material seems indisputable. The contrast between the
timid narrator and the forceful Steve reflects some of the passivity of
Hardy's own nature, whilst the enigmatic presence of the Man who
had Failed, one of the 'losers in the world's battle' (*OE*, p. 3), signals
a fundamental uneasiness at the kinds of derring-do depicted in the
tale. The action of the story, revolving as it does around the caves in
the depths of the hills, may be read as an allegory on the processes of
literary creation, processes having their source deep within the
writer's psyche. When he was dabbling in the taking of hashish,
Walter Benjamin related his experiences to the unwinding of
Ariadne's thread, finding 'joy in the mere act of unrolling a ball of
thread'. Trance is closely akin, in his account, to the process of poetic
creation which is simultaneously a discovery of the labyrinthine past:

> We go forward; but in so doing we not only discover the twists and turns
> of the cave, but also enjoy this pleasure of discovery against the back-
> ground of the other, rhythmical bliss of unwinding the thread. The
> certainty of unrolling an artfully wound skein—is that not the joy of all
> productivity, at least in prose?[3]

Benjamin's image suggests both the creative and the hermeneutic process which is embodied in the action of the boyish protagonists of *Our
Exploits at West Poley*. The explorations into the subterranean pas-
sageways beneath the Mendips, and the action of tampering with the
stream's course, implicitly represent and imagine the connection
between creativity and a search for origins which are always already
displaced. When he tried to recall the characteristically mislaid
diagrammatic representation of his life, Benjamin saw it taking the
form of a labyrinth, and noticed that the most significant feature of his

sketch was not what lay at its 'enigmatic centre' but 'the many entrances leading into the interior', each of which he designated 'primal relationships'.[4] Delving into the past, for Hardy as for Benjamin, takes the form of a kind of atavistic burrowing, a movement into what Benjamin calls 'the cool tomb of long ago, from the vault of which the present seems to return only as an echo'.[5] The overlaying of the present by a more potent past was to become a salient feature of Hardy's writing: it is here complicated by the quest for a source, an origin, undertaken by two essentially fatherless boys. Indeed the recreation of a kind of permanent boyhood necessitates excluding the female from that oral stage which Freud claimed for her. As Irigaray has pointed out, Freud's claim was significant, and yet still exiled woman from 'her most archaic and constituent site'. Woman can only function creatively, Irigaray argues, 'if she retains her relationship to the *spatial* and the *foetal*'. She is, however, deprived of these spaces by man, 'who uses them to fabricate a sense of nostalgia for this first and ultimate dwelling-place'. Man's work of acculturation (and Hardy's tale) thus takes the form of what Irigaray designates 'the endless construction of substitutes for his prenatal home'.[6]

The drama instigated by the diversion of the stream, and the interplay and rivalry of the two villages, does not mask for the reader the underlying sense of a bourgeois pathos of loss and removal from pleasure and innocence. The caves become the primal arena to which the boys return compulsively in a revealing pattern of repetition and variation, their quest for a source acting out that logocentric desire for origins which, in Derridean thought, is rendered impossible by the logic of supplementarity. Indeed, the alterations of the stream's course might aptly suggest the verbal swerve from origins of all writing. In the pleasurable text, Barthes notes, 'pornographic messages are embodied in sentences so pure they might be used as grammatical models'. The boys' redirection of the river's course makes manifest for the reader the way, in such texts, language is redistributed to create what Barthes designates two 'edges': the first edge, visibly dominant in this boys' adventure tale, is 'an obedient, conformist, plagiarising edge' in which the language 'is to be copied in its canonical state, as it has been established by schooling, good usage, literature, culture'. The opposing edge is, by contrast, 'mobile, blank (ready to assume any contours)'. While such an edge is characterized by linguistic violence, this is not the source of readerly pleasure:

'what pleasure wants is the site of a loss, the seam, the cut'.[7] *Our Exploits at West Poley* takes the form of a precise manipulation of the Barthesian edges, the level-headed schoolboy tone forming a layer which exposes the fluidity beneath. Hardy's story, with its plain-dealing transparency of utterance, seeks out an originary moment through a movement which is always baffled. The authorial impulse has been well defined by Catherine Belsey:

> longing to be the origin of language, the source of meaning and truth, to be able to inscribe the Word in the word, for ever in quest of presence, but haunted by the lack which ensures differance.[8]

Textual meaning is created not out of an originary moment but out of other texts and out of a signifying practice which, for all its transparency, Belsey observes, 'can never quite deliver the imagined plenitude of meaning-which-is-truth'.[9] In his celebration of the death of the author, Barthes defines a writing which 'traces a field without origin', embodied in language 'which ceaselessly calls into question all origins'.[10] Indeed, his description of the undermining of the role of the critic as one who deciphers texts remarkably parallels the boys' excited exploration of the caves:

> In the multiplicity of writing, everything is to be *disentangled*, nothing *deciphered*; the structure can be followed, 'run' (like the thread of a stocking) at every point and at every level, but there is nothing beneath: the space of writing is to be ranged over, not pierced; writing ceaselessly posits meaning ceaselessly to evaporate it, carrying out a systematic exemption of meaning.[11]

The constant diversion of the river from any fixed point acts out, in the unconscious of the narrative drive, Barthes's thesis that 'a text's unity lies not in its origin but in its destination'.[12] The boys wrest meaning from the fixity of authorial control; they are, in the economy of the tale, Barthesian readers, whilst the (defunct) author may be glimpsed in the faded presence of the Man who had Failed. Thus it is that, although *Our Exploits at West Poley* conforms rigidly to the decorum of the children's adventure yarn, no point of origin need be postulated. As a narrative deformation of prior narratives, Hardy's tale functions through an intertextuality which, in Barthes's words, 'is not to be confused with some origin of the text'. The boys' arbitrary action in shifting the site of the river suggests a Barthesian textual play, since 'the citations which go to make up a text are anonymous, untraceable, and yet *already read*'.[13]

The penetration effected by the boys behind the pubic screen of bushes down the 'narrow tunnel' (*OE*, p. 6) terminating in an inner cave, out of which flows a 'pellucid stream' (*OE*, p. 7), patently offers itself up to a reading which sees the story as a sexual rite of initiation. Yet the text possesses riddling qualities which might be more radically elaborated in relation to Julia Kristeva's ideas about poetic language, notably her distinction between the semiotic and the symbolic. As Toril Moi explicates it, the Kristevan semiotic is 'linked to the pre-Oedipal primary processes, the basic pulsions of which Kristeva sees as predominantly anal and oral', and these pulsations are 'gathered up in the *chora* (from the Greek word for enclosed space, womb)'.[14] Kristeva herself expounds the difficult notions involved as follows:

> Discrete quantities of energy move through the body of the subject who is not yet constituted as such and, in the course of his development, they are arranged according to the various constraints imposed on this body— always already involved in a semiotic process—by family and social structures. In this way the drives, which are 'energy' charges as well as 'psychical' marks, articulate what we call a *chora*: a non-expressive totality formed by the drives and their stases in a motility that is as full of movement as it is regulated.[15]

The *chora*, a cave-like space, is thus the site of the instinctual semiotic, preceding meaning and signification. Like the stream beneath the Mendips the semiotic is, in Kristeva's scheme, 'mobile, amorphous, but already regulated'.[16] It is not to be conceived of, as Kristeva stresses, as a 'place' somehow prior to the formation of the subject:

> Because the subject is always *both* semiotic *and* symbolic, no signifying system he produces can be either 'exclusively' semiotic or 'exclusively' symbolic, and is instead necessarily marked by an indebtedness to both.[17]

By imagining the adventures deep within the caves, it is as though Hardy is seeking the basis of his writing self, that disruptively poetic semiotic characterized by Jacqueline Rose as 'traces of the subject's difficult passage into the proper order of language'.[18] Poetic language is imbued with the semiotic, a 'distinctive mark, trace, index, precursory sign, proof, engraved or written sign', as Kristeva defines it,[19] which leads to what has been called 'the destruction of fixed, unified, constant subjectivity knotted into the sign'.[20] The boys, in their subterranean delvings, activate and release the semiotic within the womb-like inner space below the hills, and their action throws the ordered social communities above ground into chaos.

It has been argued that the role of poetic language is to place identity of meaning and the speaking subject into crisis 'because it refers
to unconscious processes, to the drives and to the socio-historical constraints in which these processes are structured'.[21] The boys' action,
first in diverting the stream to East Poley, and then in blocking all the
exits and creating the underground lake, acts out the way the 'fixed'
position of the subject in the symbolic order is undermined by poetic
language, 'shaken, if not destroyed, by the flooding in of the activity
of the drives'.[22] The tensions between the community—the miller, the
shoemaker, the farmers, the Man who had Failed—and the boys arise
out of the way, as Kristeva analyses it, discourse moves with and
against the *chora* in the sense that it simultaneously depends upon and
refuses it, producing a body which (notably in Hardy's own case) is a
site of permanent scission. The stream, rising in the cave, travels
through underground limestone caverns before emerging into day-
light. Its course mimetically reproduces the trajectory of poetic language in Kristeva's scheme:

> the moment it stops being mere instinctual glossolalia and becomes part of
> the linguistic order, poetry meets up with denotation and enunciation—
> verisimilitude and the subject—and, through them, the social.[23]

Once the subject—boy, miller, Man who had Failed, author—enters
the symbolic order, as Moi explains, the *chora* will be repressed, per-
ceptible only as a 'pulsional *pressure*' on the symbolic, 'as
contradictions, meaninglessness, disruption, silences and absences'
which 'can never be caught up in the closure of traditional linguistic
theory'.[24] It is such closure, within the dynamics of the narrative, that
Steve attempts when he employs explosives to block the opening in the
hillside:

> At a point somewhat in advance of the little gallery to the inner cave,
> Nick's Pocket ceased to exist. Its roof had sunk. The whole super-
> imposed mountain, as it seemed, had quietly settled down upon the
> hollow places beneath it, closing like a pair of bellows, and barring all
> human entrance (*OE*, p. 76).

Yet the effect here is complex, offering both closure and reopening.
Kristeva says of woman, fantasizing the collapse of the patriarchal
symbolic order, that 'She can enjoy [it] if, identifying with the
mother' she proceeds to imagine herself 'to be the sublime repressed
which returns in the fissures of the order'.[25] Hardy's art, like all

creative work, 'necessitates reinvesting the maternal *chora* so that it transgresses the symbolic order', as Kristeva puts it.[26] *Our Exploits at West Poley* embodies within its textuality the smoothness of the symbolic and the eruptive force of the semiotic, eruptions which may denote 'waves of attack against stases', but which ultimately may attest to that 'influx of the death drive'[27] represented in the flood-scene, a scene experienced by the reader as both erotic and deathly. Indeed the repetitive diversions of the stream suggest the way in which, in Kristeva's analysis, the symbolic order of language is placed 'at the service of the death drive', which 'diverts it and confines it as if within an isolated pocket of narcissism'[28] such as 'Nick's Pocket' in the story. Simultaneously with this drive towards extinction, Hardy linguistically reimagines a primal birth-scene, the move into 'the bowels of the Mendip hills' (*OE*, p. 5) providing a meta-commentary upon the way, in Kristeva's account, 'textual experience represents one of the most daring explorations the subject can allow himself, one that delves into his constitutive process'.[29] The boys' discovery of the 'nether regions' and the 'delightful recess' (*OE*, p. 7) serves as a striking manifestation of the uncovering of the maternal body which, Kristeva argues, 'the desiring subject will image as a "receptacle"', and as an allegorical treatment of the way the artist 'sketches out a kind of second birth' through the activation of poetic language.[30] Leonard's discovery of 'a low opening', 'like a human mouth, into which the stream would naturally flow' (*OE*, p. 7), commingles maternal and erotic elements in a curiously Hardyan manner. The boys' delighted digging, and their diversion of the stream by moving the 'breakwater of sand and stones' (*OE*, p. 8), triggers off that Kristevan heterogeneity of language which 'negativises all terms', 'threatening them with possible dissolution'.[31] The placing of this action within the 'range of limestone rocks' (*OE*, p. 5), with their stalactites and stalagmites, makes visible what Kristeva characterizes as the 'vertical stratification' of the symbolic order into referent, signifier and signified, and its perpetual remodelling by the 'influx of the semiotic'.[32] With its interplay between subterranean, primal and disruptive forces and the controlled regularity of signification within the social, *Our Exploits at West Poley* exemplifies the way in which, according to Barthes, each text possesses 'a multi-layering of meanings which always lets the previous meaning continue, as in a geological formation, saying the opposite without giving up the contrary'.[33] Kristeva articulates the notion of the *chora* in the following terms:

Indifferent to language, enigmatic and feminine, this space underlying the written is rhythmic, unfettered, irreducible to its intelligible verbal translation.[34]

Nevertheless, the *chora* is thought of as already regulated, just as the flow of water is controlled by Hardy's boyish protagonists. It is the place where 'the subject is both generated and negated, the place where his unity succumbs before the process of charges and stases that produce him'.[35] That there exists a dialectic between semiotic and symbolic, subterranean depths and surface, is emphasized by Rose's warning against misreading the semiotic as the 'hidden underside of culture', a force which gets 'idealised as something whose value and exuberance the culture cannot manage'.[36] The production of meaning is, rather, a question of the positioning of the subject, as Moi explains:

> The semiotic continuum must be split if signification is to be produced. This splitting (*coupure*) of the semiotic *chora* is the *thetic* phase. . . and it enables the subject to attribute differences and thus signification to what was the ceaseless heterogeneity of the *chora*.[37]

At the end of *Our Exploits at West Poley*, what Kristeva designates the 'other scene', that 'unconscious, drive-related and transverbal scene' whose 'eruptions' act as determinants of both speech and personal relations,[38] is effectively banished. The symbolic order asserts its grip in the rationalized discourse of the now significantly named Man who had Failed. The pallid advice of the village sage reveals this character's deep complicity in the act of authorship. The literary work, Barthes claims, is 'always written by a socially disappointed or powerless group'. In its refusal of its own discoveries, *Our Exploits at West Poley* elaborates the manner in which literature may be deemed 'the expression of this disappointment'.[39] The Man who had Failed stresses 'quiet perseverance' and 'clearly defined courses'; linguistic transgression, like the alteration to the course of the stream, is now closed down (*OE*, p. 78). Yet the limp triteness of the narrator's final endorsement of this homily tells a different story, as does the subsequent history of what Hardy termed his 'healthy' text for the 'intelligent youth of both sexes'.[40]

In the instability of the title (Hardy also suggested *A Tale of the Mendips*), in the hiding away of the manuscript in the filing cabinet of the *Youth's Companion*, and in its finally reaching the light of day in the suitably inappropriate context of a journal for American housewives, *Our Exploits at West Poley* stands as a paradigm of the nature of textuality and the creative process. As R.L. Purdy explains, the text went 'unnoticed and disappeared from memory',[41] like the underground caverns it seeks to describe. Such a disappearance, both deplored and willed by its creator, was only resolved by its recuperation for a wholly antipathetic reading audience in a publishing history of concealment and misreading which mirrors the dialectical relationship between the overlaying symbolic order and the disruptive rhythms of the *chora* and its emergent semiotic. Indeed, a letter which Hardy sent to his original editor explaining the purpose of his tale is revealingly couched in terms of disruption and breakage. 'The end of each chapter', Hardy claimed, 'will probably form a sufficiently striking point for breaking off the weekly instalment; but equally good places may be discovered elsewhere, if your editor should desire a different division'.[42] Towards the end of the story, the shoemaker reflects that ' "As long as that cave is known in Poley, so long will they bother us about the stream" ' (*OE*, p. 71). This comes after the 'much tantalised river' has withdrawn its 'last drop from the new channel, and reverted to its original course once more' (*OE*, p. 71). In its almost subliminal exploration of maternal spaces made over to a narrative, organizing drive which is primarily masculine (Nick's Pocket, Grim Billy), and in its quest for sources and diversions of a primal stream, *Our Exploits at West Poley* was evidently a text preternaturally destined to be lost in the cavity of an American filing-cabinet.

Notes

1. R.L. Purdy, 'Introduction', in *Our Exploits at West Poley* (Oxford: Oxford University Press, 1981), pp. vii-ix.
2. Barthes, *Pleasure of the Text*, p. 26.
3. Benjamin, *One-Way Street*, p. 220.
4. *One-Way Street*, p. 319.
5. *One-Way Street*, p. 345.
6. Irigaray, 'Sexual Difference', in Moi (ed), *French Feminist Thought*, pp. 122-23.
7. Barthes, *Pleasure of the Text*, pp. 6-7.
8. C. Belsey, *Milton* (Oxford: Basil Blackwell, 1988), p. 34.
9. Belsey, *Milton*, p. 45.
10. R. Barthes, *Image, Music, Text* (trans. S. Heath; London: Fontana, 1977), p. 146.
11. Barthes, *Image, Music, Text*, p. 147.

12. Barthes, *Image, Music, Text*, p. 148.
13. Barthes, *Image, Music, Text*, p. 160.
14. Moi, *Sexual/Textual Politics*, p. 161.
15. T. Moi (ed.), *The Kristeva Reader* (Oxford: Basil Blackwell, 1986), p. 93.
16. Moi (ed.), *Kristeva Reader*, p. 102.
17. Moi (ed.), *Kristeva Reader*, p. 93.
18. J. Rose, *Sexuality in the Field of Vision* (London: Verso, 1986), p. 144.
19. Moi (ed.), *Kristeva Reader*, p. 93.
20. R. Coward and J. Ellis, *Language and Materialism* (London: Routledge & Kegan Paul, 1977), p. 150.
21. Coward and Ellis, *Language and Materialism*, p. 148.
22. Coward and Ellis, *Language and Materialism*, p. 148.
23. Moi (ed.), *Kristeva Reader*, p. 110.
24. Moi, *Sexual/Textual Politics*, p. 162.
25. Kristeva, cited in Gallop, *Feminism and Psychoanalysis*, p. 123.
26. Moi (ed.), *Kristeva Reader*, p. 115.
27. Moi (ed.), *Kristeva Reader*, pp. 95, 103.
28. Moi (ed.), *Kristeva Reader*, p. 119.
29. Moi (ed.), *Kristeva Reader*, p. 117.
30. Moi (ed.), *Kristeva Reader*, pp. 128, 120.
31. Moi (ed.), *Kristeva Reader*, p. 108.
32. Moi (ed.), *Kristeva Reader*, p. 113.
33. Barthes, *Image, Music, Text*, p. 58.
34. Moi (ed.), *Kristeva Reader*, p. 97.
35. Moi (ed.), *Kristeva Reader*, p. 95.
36. Rose, *Sexuality*, p. 154.
37. Moi, *Sexual/Textual Politics*, pp. 161-62.
38. Moi (ed.), *Kristeva Reader*, p. 153.
39. Barthes, *Pleasure of the Text*, p. 39.
40. Letter of 5 April 1883, cited in R.L. Purdy, *Thomas Hardy: A Bibliographical Study* (Oxford: Clarendon Press, 1978), p. 302.
41. Purdy, *Thomas Hardy*, p. 303.
42. Letter of 5 November 1883, in Purdy, *Thomas Hardy*, p. 302.

Chapter 4

THREE SHORT STORIES (1891–93)

1. *'On the Western Circuit'*

'On the Western Circuit' was written in the autumn of 1891, and a somewhat bowdlerized version published in *The English Illustrated Magazine* at the end of that year. Hardy subsequently revised and expanded the story, and it was published in its final form in *Life's Little Ironies* three years later. The story concerns a young barrister, Charles Raye, who falls in love with Anna, a country girl, in the cathedral city of Melchester, while practising on the western legal circuit. Raye returns to London, but continues to write to Anna at the house of Mrs Harnham, for whom she works. Anna is illiterate, and Mrs Harnham, who is trapped in a loveless marriage with an elderly wine merchant, undertakes to reply to Raye's letters on the girl's behalf. When Anna finds herself pregnant, Mrs Harnham composes a letter of such tact and delicacy that Raye determines to marry the servant-girl. Anna leaves Melchester, and Edith Harnham continues to correspond more passionately than ever. She accompanies Anna to London for the wedding. After the ceremony, Raye discovers that Anna is illiterate, and that 'in soul and spirit' he has married Mrs Harnham, whose thoughts centre obsessively upon him as she finally returns to her husband in Melchester. As the Rayes travel to their honeymoon destination, Charles's sole comfort lies in perusing the letters signed by 'Anna'.

As Kristin Brady remarks, in the stories which make up *Life's Little Ironies* the narrative voice is significantly heard, teaching the reader 'to interpret events from a particular perspective'. These events, Brady points out, largely occur 'among the respectable middle classes to which many of Hardy's readers belonged'. The tragi-comic working up of episodes of provincial life is produced not by a simple determinism, but through what Brady terms 'the dramatic interaction

of persons and society, of character and environment'. The protagonists of 'On the Western Circuit' are stock types: Raye is an 'end-of-
the-age young man' (*DP*, p. 252), Anna a 'pretty rural maiden' (*DP*,
p. 253), and Edith Harnham an unhappy young wife, a 'lonely,
impressionable creature' (*DP*, p. 252) who observes the goings-on in
the city from her drawing-room window. Brady demonstrates how
these stereotypes 'illuminate the manner in which instinctive sexual
needs are modified, and even defined, by social and intellectual expectations', and she goes on to show how, through the letter-writing,
Edith seeks increasingly 'to restore in herself the youth she has lost in
her marriage'.[1]

A productive way into this tricky story may be provided by Hillis
Miller's critique of a Hardy poem, 'The Torn Letter'. The speaker
begins the poem by tearing his beloved's letter 'into strips':

> In darkness on my bed alone
>   I seemed to see you in a vision,
>   And hear you say: 'Why this derision
> Of one drawn to you, though unknown?'

Soon enough, however, night cools the speaker's 'hasty madness', and
brings about a 'real remorse':

> Uprising then, as things unpriced
>   I sought each fragment, patched and mended;
>   The midnight whitened ere I had ended
> And gathered words I had sacrificed.

Not all the fragments may be recuperated:

> But some, alas, of those I threw
>   Were past my search, destroyed for ever:
>   They were your name and place; and never
> Did I regain those clues to you.

The Will, it appears, had determined that the pair 'should be divided':

> That ache for you, born long ago,
>   Throbs on: I never could outgrow it.
>   What a revenge, did you but know it!
> But that, thank God, you do not know (*CP*, pp. 313-14).

Hillis Miller founds his reading of the poem upon the distinction
between speech and writing, presence and absence. He cites Kafka's
account of the mysterious business of letter-writing as an 'intercourse
with ghosts'; 'not only with the ghost of the recipient', Kafka

ruminates, 'but also with one's own ghost which develops between the lines of the letter one is writing'. Kafka goes on, in terms which illuminate the epistolary relationship of Edith Harnham and Charles Raye, to note how this 'ghost' develops a more urgent life 'in a series of letters where one letter corroborates the other and can refer to it as a witness'. 'Written kisses don't reach their destination, rather they are drunk on the way by the ghosts.' Hillis Miller glosses this notion:

> Thinking and holding are here opposed to writing. The former belongs to 'the real world' of persons, bodies, and minds, of distance and proximity. If a person is near, one can touch him, kiss him (or her). If a person is distant one can think of that person.[2]

By contrast, the apparently unproblematic act of writing is 'an extension of the terrible power of dislocation involved in the simplest "gesture" of writing a note to a friend'.[3] Behind such an account lies Derrida's complex unravelling of that speech/writing binary opposition which he detects at the heart of Western discourse. The notion that spoken language authenticates self-presence is challenged and subverted in deconstruction, where the logocentric exaltation of speech over writing is dismantled. Metaphors of writing and textual inscription disturb and disrupt every projected identification of speech and meaning. Against the tradition that writing has always been secondary, a parasitic mode of communication, Derrida argues that speech is always non-coincidental with a speaker's original intentions, and that non-coincidence is registered in the irretrievably graphic character of linguistic interchange. When the present does not 'present itself' (as when Raye returns to the metropolis) then the act of signification begins. The word is the sign of the Derridean 'deferred presence', since the signified concept is never present in itself within a language system posited upon difference. Every concept is necessarily inscribed in a chain of signification, as Raye and Anna are 'chained' to each other (*DP*, p. 268) at the end of Hardy's tale. Language is thus conceived as a written system of signifiers which, as it were, surrounds any act of speech. Neither speech nor writing takes priority; both exist solely in dialectical interdependence, and are inevitably caught up in the metaphoricity which characterizes all language.

As Hillis Miller remarks, Derrida has postulated that a letter actually 'creates the self appropriate to itself', doing 'the utmost violence on the already existing self of the hapless person who. . . reads the letter'.[4] Derrida argues thus, in his essay 'Télépathie':

Then you say: it is I, uniquely I who can receive this letter; not that it is
meant especially for me, on the contrary, but I receive as a present the
happenstance to which this card exposes itself. It chooses me. And I
choose that it should choose me by chance, I wish to cross its trajectory, I
wish to encounter myself there.

Derrida concludes, 'one cannot say of the recipient that he exists
before the letter'.[5] If Charles Raye, 'a man not altogether typical of
the middle-class male' (*DP*, p. 245), were a philosopher he might
have reasoned thus. As a character in fiction he does not exist prior to
the text in which he appears. At the fair in Melchester he is, in a
sense, uncreated, a *voyeur* or perhaps a Baudelairean *flâneur*, strolling
amusedly about the lurid spectacle. In the 'circuit' of the story he
begins neutral, empty, a void; but at the end, when the author of the
letters stands revealed to him, he bursts into life, telling Edith,
' "Why, you and I are friends—lovers—devoted lovers—by correspondence!" ' (*DP*, p. 267). Such 'correspondence' wittily signals
elective affinity as well as postal connection. In 'soul and spirit', Raye
acknowledges to Edith, ' "I have married you, and no other woman in
the world" ' (*DP*, p. 267). The two are complicit in denying an identity to the servant-girl, and their bonding merely affirms that class-
affiliation which has fuelled the story through their easy command of
a written culture. Anna stands at the centre of the triangle, her sexual
exploitation by Raye mirrored by her economic exploitation in the
Harnham household. Within the economy of the tale the working class
is silenced so that middle-class romance can articulate its own
concerns. Edith is the literal (and literate) author of the lawyer's
being, just as he is the ray(e) of light for which she searches from her
provincial window. Awakened into a life of emotion at the close, Raye
is 'chained to work for the remainder of his life', 'tied up' like the
bundle of letters he finally re-reads in the railway compartment (*DP*,
p. 268); the moment of revelatory communion and 'authentic' speech
between the middle-class lovers is also, in the Hardyan economy, the
moment of rupture. The introductory narrative indicates that Raye
'had knowledge' of both women (*DP*, p. 244), but the sexual
connotations of this remark are progressively emptied out by the
literariness of the hero's relationships.

    At the beginning of the story the narrator places Edith in the
unsurprising situation of the middle-class woman gazing out at the
hurly-burly of life. This 'dark-eyed, thoughtful' figure looks

'absently' at the weird scene of the fair, until interrupted by her husband:

> 'O, Edith, I didn't see you,' he said, 'Why are you sitting in the dark?'
> 'I am looking at the fair,' replied the lady in a languid voice.
> 'Oh? Horrid nuisance every year! I wish it could be put a stop to.'
> 'I like it.'
> 'H'm. There's no accounting for taste.' (*DP*, p. 249).

Such an exchange neatly adumbrates the way the story will issue out of a conventionally Bovaryesque marital situation, the nature of which is registered by the differing reactions to the carnival, proletarian hints of libidinal energy located in the fairground. When Raye, after his successful dalliance with Anna, returns to London, he pens 'a short, encouraging line or two, signed with his pseudonym', and receipt of this missive causes the blushing Anna to demand of the postman, '"It is mine?"' (*DP*, p. 255). Her illiteracy leads her to ask her mistress to compose a letter on her behalf, and the imposture begins. Anna's predicament illustrates the impossibility of her class and gender position within a discourse which seeks to censor the problematic question of female desire; she literally possesses no language which would enable her to insert herself into such a discourse. Her own desire is effaced and silenced in favour of the feminine as sexual content; the assertion of Anna's identity and sexuality appears to threaten the dominant discourse which is mirrored and created in the fixity and decorum of the written letters. Raye, on the other hand, as a practitioner of law, is inured to the dwindling of feeling into document which such a practice presupposes, and which enables an immobilizing and distancing of female claims to selfhood. The barrister stands within a mastering discourse, though in the Hardyan irony of the tale he is finally mastered by it. The narrative begins by Raye's picking out Anna from a number of attractive women at a fairground, his eyes centring 'on the prettiest girl out of the several pretty ones revolving' (*DP*, p. 246). His choice of partner is arbitrary, the matter of an idle moment. Woman is thus perceived as an absolute category which guarantees male identity; the girl, representing both what the man is not, and the pleasure which as a man of law he must renounce, is the basis and object of Raye's fantasy. It is a seminal moment familiar to the Hardy reader.

Edith Harnham commences by addressing an unknown correspondent, identified only by the initials 'C.B.'. The first letter, we are told,

written in Anna's presence, and 'in a measure indited by the young
girl', gains its 'life', 'spirit' and 'individuality' from the older woman,
and it is significant that Anna shrinks from writing her signature (*DP*,
p. 257). The commencement of this epistolary activity may correspond to the 'scene of writing', and it is to be repeated over the course
of the next few months. It is one of the curious features of 'On the
Western Circuit' that the contents of the letters are invisible to the
reader of the tale, who must make do with summary indications of
their drift:

> They were her own impassioned and pent-up ideas—lowered to mono-
> syllabic phraseology in order to keep up the disguise—that Edith put into
> letters signed with another name, much to the shallow Anna's delight,
> who, unassisted, could not for the world have conceived such pretty
> fancies for winning him, even had she been able to write them. Edith
> found that it was these, her own foisted-in sentiments, to which the young
> barrister mainly responded. The few sentences occasionally added from
> Anna's own lips made apparently no impression upon him (*DP*, pp. 258-
> 59).

The letters remain, thus, perpetually out of reach, representations for
both narrator and reader of an irrecoverable lack, symbols of a permanently opaque structure of exchange which takes Anna for its
absent centre. The reader of the letters, and of the tale, unwittingly
enters a signifying chain in which meaning and symbol never coin-
cide. The act of impersonation reaches such a height that, when
Anna's pregnancy is revealed (a development excised from the serial-
ized version), Edith will exclaim, ' "I wish his child was mine—I wish
it was!" ' (*DP*, p. 260). The gestation and composition of the letters
mirror this wished-for pregnancy, the body of the peasant girl being
suppressed and replaced by the 'impassioned and pent-up ideas' (*DP*,
p. 258) of the middle-class impersonator. Thomas Docherty, discussing the Aristotelian doctrine of imitation, suggests that to imper-
sonate another 'is to question the very individuality of the person thus
duplicated'. The act of impersonation offers the possibility that there
is 'no essential or natural self':

> When one person stops imitating or impersonating another, she or he does
> not return to an authentic selfhood, but returns instead to an impersonation
> of the 'originary' self. This is to say, in fact, that the impersonator has no
> self; like a Sartrean waiter, she or he can only play the role of the self,
> now simply one role among many.[6]

Edith is compelled, in the circular economy of the story, to revert to a role of wifehood which she has now virtually forgotten how to play. Docherty's observation that in such artful imitation 'an essential nature gives way entirely to the play and pleasure of art'[7] illuminates the way Edith creates her own 'story' and drains Anna of 'personality'. Hardy here covertly dramatizes both the playful excitation and demoralizing dependency of literary creativity and the class exploitation inherent in the situation. The reader must fill in the blank space by composing the summarized letters for herself; in this way such a reader becomes complicit in Edith's forgery, partial author of the tale, filling in the gaps in the text and participating in the drama of misrecognition which unfolds. In Western thought, writing has been given the function of a supplement to speech, a substitute for full presence. But such supplementarity denotes an originary absence; presence is always in fact deferred, the supplement denoting a fundamental lack. The inauguration of meaning therefore depends upon the materiality of a writing which marks the disappearance of natural presence. Meaning is always both determined and undermined by the slippage of language. The act of letter-writing in the story is a means of deferral and postponement through which both the characters and the narrative are constituted. Life protects itself by repetition and deferral: when Charles Raye receives his first letter from Melchester the narrator observes that he 'was not anxious to open the epistle', preferring instead to anticipate 'its terms of passionate retrospect and tender adjuration' (*DP*, p. 254). The act of writing erases the dangerous possibilities of presence.

The structure of 'On the Western Circuit' may be posited as a triangle in which, somewhat atypically for Hardy, two women of different classes compete for the favours of one man. Yet it is not, of course, strictly triangular: there is another voice which is heard, that of the narrator. The triangle, stock-in-trade of romantic fiction and the well-made play, is thus problematized by a fourth participant, the narrator. In the act of voicing the story the narrator duplicates the activity of Edith Harnham. Indeed, in some sense Edith is a secondary narrator, composing a narrative in accordance with her own hidden desires. Edith possesses a mastery of the situation denied both to the illiterate Anna and to the duped Charles Raye, and her letters are the exercise of that mastery. She doubles the voice of the narrator, just as the young couple are doubled in the predicament of their differing blindness.

'On the Western Circuit' is an exercise in duplicity which mirrors the very act of story-telling. In another (mis-)reading the two women may be seen as doubles, representing a misogynistic type of mind/ body duality, leaving the barrister and the narrator united in distance, knowledge and male potency of utterance. The women in the tale symptomatically experience life as a lack, an absence inscribed in the very structure of the narrative drive. It is significant of the sexual politics which are silently evoked that, when the pregnancy is discovered, Anna/Edith tells Raye/Bradford that she wishes 'above everything to be no weight upon him in his career, no clog upon his high activities' (*DP*, p. 259). Edith's action in taking up the pen to write upon the blank sheet may be read as the female equivalent of Raye's penetration of the virginal Anna. The absent texts of the letters produce a gap at the heart of the story which mirrors the blankness and absence in the participants and even at times in the narrator; when Anna is impelled to leave the household, for instance, the narrator cannot determine whether or not this is because news of her pregnancy has reached Mr Harnham (*DP*, p. 260). The legal circuit of the title, wherein the hero moves restlessly from one provincial centre to another, reproduces the unfulfillable circuit of sexual desire which links and separates the protagonists. Raye seeks an Anna who is transformed into Edith and thus unattainable: Edith desires Raye but is trapped in a loveless marriage; Anna, the original object of desire, is abandoned emotionally at the moment of apparently attaining her own desire. The counterfeiting involved in the composition of the sequence of letters is an act which implicitly acknowledges the loss which is always already embodied in writing. The writing of a letter, presupposing distance and division, falsely imagines an alternative state. It privileges speech and presence as an authentic but lost mode of being, a privileging which Hardy, as writer, frequently both acquiesces in and denies. In chapter 14 of *The Mayor of Casterbridge*, for instance, Hardy remarks how the 'old crude *viva voce* system of Henchard, in which everything depended upon his memory, and bargains were made by the tongue alone', is swept away by the 'letters and ledgers' instituted by Farfrae.

Edith's letters, we may suppose, arrive at their correct destination, and are there (mis-)read, in the same way as the story itself may be (mis-)interpreted by the reader. The slippage of identity inherent in the Anna/Edith signature serves to unravel positivist assumptions about the possibility of coherent character-drawing in nineteenth-century fiction. As in *Jude the Obscure*, Hardy in this tale stands on the threshold of modernism, with its vacillating characters and creative instability of effect. The story which the narrator recounts functions entirely through acts of substitution which interrogate certainties of identity and authentic feeling:

> Thus it befell that Edith Harnham found herself in the strange position of having to correspond, under no supervision by the real woman, with a man not her husband, in terms which were virtually those of a wife, concerning a corporeal condition that was not Edith's at all; the man being one for whom, mainly through the sympathies involved in playing this part, she secretly cherished a predilection, subtle and imaginative truly, but strong and absorbing (*DP*, p. 261).

The effect of 'On the Western Circuit' is radically to unsettle the reader's presuppositions about reading and writing. On the final page we are presented with two inverted mirror-images. In the first, Edith regretfully returns by train to Melchester. Mr Harnham (a significant absence in the serial, where Edith is a widow) misses her at the station:

> In the course of half an hour a figure opened the door of the apartment.
> 'Ah—who's that?' she said, starting up, for it was dark.
> 'Your husband—who should it be?' said the worthy merchant.
> 'Ah—my husband!—I forgot I had a husband!' she whispered to herself.
> 'I missed you at the station', he continued. 'Did you see Anna safely tied up? I hope so, for 'twas time.'
> 'Yes—Anna is married.' (*DP*, p. 268).

Simultaneously, in a train speeding towards Knollsea, the newly-weds sit in an uncomfortable silence while Charles peruses his love-letters:

> 'What are you doing, dear Charles?' she said timidly from the other window, and drew nearer to him as if he were a god.
> 'Reading over all those sweet letters to me signed "Anna"', he replied with dreary resignation (*DP*, p. 269).

A story which begins in the convivial moment of the fair ends in an enclosed and silent space of entrapment.

'On the Western Circuit' may itself be read as a kind of letter, an open letter from author to reader. A story in which a woman impersonating a second woman addresses a man known by pseudonymous initials problematizes the very act of interpretation upon which the reader is engaged. The meaning can lie only in the text, but that text, like the letters it purports to describe, remains opaque. The final recognition of the lovers is also inevitably a moment of concealment, a blindness in which the reader is implicated. 'On the Western Circuit' is a text which registers a seeping away of bodily passion into verbal expression; the body and its drives are marginalized, energy and sexuality contained by, and tamed into, textuality. Edith's displacement of desire into an endlessly inventive discursivity, a bodiless speech, acts out that primacy of textuality. Her writing is a bid for authority and a threat to the patriarchal mediation of power wielded by Harnham and Raye. In her dangerous inventiveness Edith begins to challenge the construction of womanhood epitomized by Anna's seduction. In a sense, her writings cover up the gap which the (absent) seduction makes in the text. In this story Hardy produces his *dénouement* through a scrupulously ironized reversal in which speech stands revealed as belated supplement to writing.

At the beginning of the story the fairground erupts as spectacular carnival, a riotous upsetting of proprieties in the staidly Trollopian purlieus of Melchester:

> [Raye] might have searched Europe over for a greater contrast between juxtaposed scenes. The spectacle was that of the eighth chasm of the Inferno as to colour and flame, and, as to mirth, a development of the Homeric heaven. A smoky glare, of the complexion of brass-filings, ascended from the fiery tongues of innumerable naptha lamps affixed to booths, stalls, and other temporary erections which crowded the spacious market-square. In front of this irradiation scores of human figures, more or less in profile, were darting athwart and across, up, down, and around, like gnats against a sunset (*DP*, pp. 244-45).

There is an underlying tension in the prose here which is familiar to the reader of Hardy; self-conscious straining after classical effects blends uneasily with a vigorous demotic. Yet that ponderous reaching back to the classics as the measure of the modern nicely mirrors the consciousness of the Victorian man of law, and the temporary nature of the fairground 'erections' becomes wittily proleptic of his brief dalliance. Searching for Anna, Edith Harnham descends from her isolation and finds herself unwittingly 'pressed against Anna's acquaintance'. She feels a man's hand 'clasping her fingers' as Raye squeezes what he mistakenly supposes to be the hand of his new friend (*DP*, p. 250). The drama of mistaken identity upon which the tale depends begins, therefore, in a moment of passionate corporeality. As the story proceeds, the characters retreat from this carnivalesque confusion into the discrete spaces of the sexual and social hierarchy. Bourgeois society substitutes for the corporeal body the literary body of the text—the letters, the narrator's story. The moment of passional misrecognition and desire is fragmented and displaced into writing, distance and class division.

In the course of their dissection of bourgeois hysteria and the carnivalesque, Peter Stallybrass and Allon White provide a productive context for this scene. The 'horrid nuisance' of the fair is something Mr Harnham wishes could be stopped (*DP*, p. 249), and this censorious ambition reflects the historical suppression of fairs, wakes and other symptoms of the carnivalesque by the middle class throughout Europe, as Stallybrass and White explain:

> This act of disavowal on the part of the emergent bourgeoisie, with its sentimentalism and its disgust, *made* carnival into the festival of the Other. It encoded all that which the proper bourgeois must strive *not to be* in order to preserve a stable and 'correct' sense of self.[8]

This festival of carnivalesque impropriety erupts most potently in Hardy in the skimmington ride which originates in the 'low' area of Mixen Lane in *The Mayor of Casterbridge*. At the same time the marginalizing repression of social function led to a process of displacement into bourgeois practice; carnivalesque qualities lurk within discourse to the extent that the transmutation of carnival can never be characterized simply as the imposition of censorship. On the contrary, the process involves 'tracing migrations, concealment, metamorphoses, fragmentations, internalisation and neurotic sublimations'[9] of the kind epitomized in Edith's letter-writing. The female bourgeois subject, Stallybrass and White observe, was placed 'on the outside of a grotesque carnival body which is articulated as social pleasure and celebration', a body which attacks egotistical authority and flaunts its libidinal materiality.[10] Thus Edith Harnham watches the fair at Melchester, first from her drawing-room and later from a 'screened nook' in the square (*DP*, p. 250) which enables her to spy on the lovers. The hysterical middle-class woman of the late-Victorian period, both site and victim of psychoanalytic practice, was culturally produced by her inability to name or direct her own physicality and sexuality—disturbing features imaged in the erotic movement of the fairground machines and their customers:

> Their motions were so rhythmical that they seemed to be moved by machinery. And it presently appeared that they were moved by machinery indeed; the figures being those of the patrons of swings, see-saws, flying-leaps, above all the three steam roundabouts which occupied the centre of

the position. It was from the latter that the din of steam-organs came (*DP*,
p. 245).

From this scene Charles Raye is as alienated as Mrs Harnham. Unlike
the 'majority of the crowd', he wanders in isolation through the
'gyrating personages' of the steam-circus (*DP*, p. 245), until he spots
the country girl, 'absolutely unconscious of everything save the act of
riding', her features 'rapt in an ecstatic dreaminess' (*DP*, p. 246).
Raye is full of 'vague latter-day glooms and popular melancholies'
(*DP*, p. 246) from which the sexually enraptured young girl, locked
into carnivalesque embrace, will deliver him. The moment is archetypal, as the general analysis of Stallybrass and White serves to indicate:

> There is no more easily recognisable scene of bourgeois pathos than the
> lonely crowd in which individual identity is achieved *over against* all the
> others, through the sad realisation of not-belonging. That moment, in
> which the subject is made the outsider to the crowd, an onlooker,
> compensating for exclusion through the deployment of the discriminating
> gaze, is at the very root of bourgeois sensibility.[11]

The fairground locates and celebrates the body and represents an
otherness, a proletarian energy and culture, from which Raye and
Edith are cut off; that separation is classically formulated in the
repressed hysteria of the mutually interchanged letters.

After Raye has conversed with Anna, the roundabout begins again,
carrying the girl with it:

> Then the pleasure-machine started again, and, to the lighthearted girl, the
> figure of the handsome young man, the market-square with its lights and
> crowd, the houses beyond, and the world at large began moving round as
> before, counter-moving in the revolving mirrors on her right hand, she
> being as it were the fixed point in an undulating, dazzling, lurid universe,
> in which loomed forward most prominently of all the form of her late
> interlocutor (*DP*, pp. 247-48).

The spatial relationship between the girl, a point of fixity amidst the
dazzling mirrors, and the reflected form of her 'late interlocutor' is
proleptic: 'Each time that she approached the half of her orbit that lay
nearest him they gazed at each other with smiles' (*DP*, p. 248). There
is here an optical repetition of Raye's 'double' reflected and refracted
in the revolving mirror, so that the eye of the girl must in a sense
generate both his identity and the 'dazzling, lurid universe' (*DP*,
p. 248) through which she revolves. An erotic charge connects the
light, the crowds and the solitary figure in a chain of metaphorical

transformations. The mirrored image suggests the range of illusion and misrecognition which will be exploited in the composition of letters. The confusions of vision inherent in the novel experience of the crowded fairground were, in Benjamin's trenchant analysis, features peculiar to the middle of the nineteenth century. The 'daily sight of a lively crowd', he reflects, 'may once have constituted a spectacle to which one's eyes had to adapt first'. Hardy's description of the light and movement of the fair serves as a prose parallel to the impressionist technique whereby, as Benjamin puts it, 'the picture is garnered in a riot of dabs of colour'.[12] Writing, 'On the Western Circuit' declares, involves censorship. As he had frequently done in his novels, Hardy produced a pre-censored magazine version, bereft of both Anna's pregnancy and Edith's husband, and later a more challenging version for book publication. The story, thus conceived and written, possessed no finality, contaminated in its very inception by the class-complicity and antagonism of author and reader. In the act of writing, identity gives way to representation. The bodies of the lovers are now, as it were, supplementary to the cultural process of signification within which they are caught up; their final meeting is both a revelation and an embarrassment from which they retreat. Sexual desire, reinscribed in the literary artefacts which are the letters, lurks within the discourse like a troubled ghost, leaving the reader, like Edith Harnham, trapped in an 'impassioned dream' (*DP*, p. 268); located within, yet inevitably exiled from, the body and its desires.

2. *'An Imaginative Woman'*

While 'An Imaginative Woman' (1893) deals with a typical Hardyan situation centring upon marital unhappiness, baulked feelings and lost opportunities, the atmosphere of stifling emotion is remarkably held and focused. The Marchmills are an ill-assorted couple, William being a bluff, pragmatic Midlands gunmaker, his wife Ella, by contrast, an 'impressionable, palpitating creature' (*DP*, p. 306) who releases her frustrations in verse. On holiday at Solentsea, they take rooms on the front. In order to accommodate them the landlady lets them have the apartment of a young poet, Robert Trewe, who temporarily moves across to the Isle of Wight. Ella, who writes her poems under the pseudonym of 'John Ivy', has long been an admirer of Trewe's more forceful verse. Living in his rooms she becomes obsessed with Trewe and hopes to meet him, but he fails to call when expected. She gazes raptly at the poet's photograph, which the phlegmatic Marchmill later discovers. Although Ella prolongs her stay at Solentsea, the poet remains elusive. Returning home, she begins to correspond with him under her male pseudonym. When she discovers that a mutual friend is on a walking tour with Trewe, she invites the pair to call; once again the poet fails to materialize, depressed by a negative review of his latest volume. Shortly afterwards, the newspapers carry the news of Trewe's suicide, and a letter read out at the inquest reveals the poet's longing for a sympathetic female companion. Ella obtains a lock of the poet's hair and his picture, and secretly visits the grave on the day of the funeral, pursued by her husband. Some months afterwards she dies in childbirth, having revealed her love for Trewe. Two years later, contemplating remarriage, Marchmill comes across the lock of hair and the photograph, and is struck by the resemblance between Trewe and his youngest child, whom he now angrily rejects.

Although 'An Imaginative Woman' is based upon an earlier sketch, the story as it stands owes something to Hardy's involvement with the Hon. Mrs Florence Henniker during the early 1890s. Hardy, who refers directly to Shelley in the tale and twice quotes from *Prometheus Unbound*, regarded the aristocratic young woman as an avatar of the poet. He encouraged her writing, of which he arranged reviews, and collaborated with her on a short story entitled 'The Spectre of the Real'. In July 1893 Hardy visited Florence in Southsea (Solentsea), where her husband, Major Henniker, was then stationed; on 14 September he sent off the manuscript of 'An Imaginative Woman'. In this manuscript Trewe is given the name Crewe, which was the maiden name of Florence Henniker's mother. While Trewe's death probably owes something to myths about the demise of Keats, the poet is, as Millgate observes, 'strikingly similar to Hardy himself in his extreme sensitivity to unfair criticism'.[13] The reference to Trewe's 'mournful ballad on "Severed Lives"' (*DP*, p. 315) suggests Hardy's poem 'The Division', prompted by his feelings for Mrs Henniker:

> O were it but the weather, Dear,
>   O were it but the miles
> That summed up all our severance,
>   There might be room for smiles.
>
> But that thwart thing betwixt us twain,
>   Which nothing cleaves or clears,

Is more than distance, Dear, or rain,
And longer than the years! (*CP*, p. 221).

Millgate pertinently traces the connection between Ella/Florence
revealed by 'the militariness of her surname, by her husband's occu-
pation of "gunmaker", and by the use of Solentsea (i.e. Southsea) as a
setting'.[14]

'An Imaginative Woman' explores the kind of unrequited love
which Hardy's imagination found most potent. Mrs Henniker's allure
was consonant with her distance and her marital status. While
Marchmill characteristically speaks in 'squarely shaped sentences'
(*DP*, p. 306), his wife is differently imagined:

Her figure was small, elegant, and slight in build, tripping, or rather
bounding, in movement. She was dark-eyed, and had that marvellously
bright and liquid sparkle in each pupil which characterises persons of
Ella's cast of soul, and is too often a cause of heartache to the possessor's
male friends, ultimately sometimes to herself (*DP*, p. 306).

Ella's relationship with Trewe is, from the first, that of slave to
master. Trewe's work, 'impassioned rather than ingenious' (*DP*,
p. 309), is, she feels, 'so much stronger' than 'her own feeble lines'
(*DP*, p. 310). Ella, who pays for the publication of her own verses,
adopts the masculine pseudonym, 'John Ivy'; her relationship with the
elusive Trewe is both parasitic and self-destructive, as her adopted
surname suggests. Hardy had alluded to such relationships in his poem
'The Ivy-Wife':

In new affection next I strove
To coll an ash I saw,
And he in trust received my love;
Till with my soft green claw
I cramped and bound him as I wove. . .
Such was my love: ha-ha!

By this I gained his strength and height
Without his rivalry.
But in my triumph I lost sight
Of afterhaps. Soon he,
Being bark-bound, flagged, snapped, fell outright,
And in his fall felled me! (*CP*, p. 57).

John Ivy's book 'fell dead in a fortnight' (*DP*, p. 310), its feebleness
explicitly contrasted with Trewe's powerful utterance. Inspecting the
room inhabited previously by her idol, Ella notices some 'minute

scribblings in pencil on the wall-paper behind the curtains at the head of the bed' (*DP*, p. 311). This pre-text, which comes to obsess the admiring woman, takes the form of what Derrida has called 'a topography of traces'; it is a record of the creative psyche. As Derrida argues,

> The unconscious text is already a weave of pure traces, differences in which meaning and force are united—a text nowhere present, consisting of archives which are *always already* transcriptions.

Such traces, thus, are 'repositories of a meaning which was never present, whose signified presence is always reconstituted by deferral'.[15] Repetition, trace and deferral are the defining characteristics of Trewe's art and of Hardy's story: the poet absents himself from his rooms to enable the Marchmills to spend their holiday there; he fails to call as arranged with his landlady; when Ella crosses to the Isle of Wight, she is unable to locate the writer's cottage with any certainty; Trewe moves back to the mainland, but still does not materialize; when Ella, ensconced in her own home again, finally invites him to call, he once again disappears at the last moment; his final disappearance is announced in the newspaper. Ella's emotions luxuriate under this perpetual absence; she immerses herself in Trewe's 'half-obliterated pencillings' (*DP*, p. 317), and gazes raptly at his photograph. 'The repression of writing', Derrida argues, is 'the repression of that which threatens presence and the mastering of absence'.[16]

The two seminal moments in 'An Imaginative Woman' focus intensely upon this absence. In the first, Ella dons a mackintosh belonging to Trewe, and gazes at her reflection in the mirror:

> Possessed of her fantasy, Ella went later in the afternoon, when nobody was in that part of the house, opened the closet, unhitched one of the articles, a mackintosh, and put it on, with the waterproof cap belonging to it.
> 'The mantle of Elijah!' she said. 'Would it might inspire me to rival him, glorious genius that he is!'
> Her eyes always grew wet when she thought like that, and she turned to look at herself in the glass. *His* heart had beat inside that coat, and *his* brain had worked under that hat at levels of thought she would never reach. The consciousness of her weakness beside him made her feel quite sick (*DP*, p. 313).

In its depiction of the female donning the overcoat, a garment identified in Freudian dream-symbolism with the male sexual organ, the text imagines and places the hysterical woman seeking to obliterate her otherness, as her poetry has already been obliterated by male writing. As Jane Gallop observes, 'Women need to reach "the same": that is, be "like men", able to represent themselves'. In a heterosexual encounter (or, as here, non-encounter) the woman 'will always be engulfed', unable 'to represent her difference'.[17] Because poet and disciple never meet, the effect is of a prolonged courtship. Gallop remarks, 'the law which prohibits sexual intercourse between analyst and patient actually makes the seduction last forever'.[18] The mirror gives back to Ella an image of herself disguised as Trewe, just as her epistolary admiration and undeclared love serve as a mirror for the poet's desire. Thus does the woman, in Gallop's analysis, end up 'functioning as mirror, giving back a coherent, framed representation to the appropriately masculine subject'.[19] Freud postulated that hysterics had fantasies which arose out of both hetero- and homosexual impulse. Male psychoanalytical theory, indeed, suggests that the fundamental question for the hysteric is one of sexual identity, and it is precisely this theorization which feminism has sought to challenge. The female hysterical subject, it is argued, is prone to imitation and submission because of the ideological position offered to women by discourse—in this case, the competing but complementary middle-class male discourses of business and art. Ella stands trapped between subjection and revolt; confronted by the signifier 'woman' she is finally of no account to Trewe, Marchmill or even the narrator. Compelled to obliteration, Ella must literally forget herself. The 'half-obliterated' inscriptions which Trewe leaves on the bedroom wallpaper are sufficiently powerful to cause this self-abnegation. Freud's account of hysterical amnesia is germane:

> Hysterical amnesia, which occurs at the bidding of repression, is only explicable by the fact that the subject is already in possession of a store of memory-traces which have been withdrawn from conscious disposal, and which are now, by an associative link, attracting to themselves the material which the forces of repression are engaged in repelling from consciousness.[20]

Ella is drawn into an echoic creativity of utterance which is both permitted (as it were in the Imaginary) and denied (by the symbolic order) by the discovery of these traces. The writing which marks Trewe's absence is the most dominating form of presence for the woman. It is important to insist, nonetheless, that within this general situation of dominance/submission, Ella still finds her own voice and expresses a genuine creativity. Elaine Showalter argues, in this connection, that the hysterical woman was a type of 'feminist heroine, fighting back against confinement in the bourgeois home'. Hysteria, understood thus, may be read as 'a mode of protest for women deprived of other social or intellectual outlets or expressive options'.[21]

Ella discovers in Robert Trewe what no one else finds; she recognizes the absence in his name and is alert to that in him which his name does not name. The pair are, as it were, names emptied of solidity. The encounter of two absences which so beguiles Hardy is thus dependent upon the act of writing. In the second climactic scene Ella contemplates both the poet's photograph and the traces of his handwriting:

> she set up the photograph on its edge upon the coverlet, and contemplated it as she lay. Then she scanned again by the light of the candle the half-obliterated pencillings on the wallpaper beside her head. There they were—phrases, couplets, *bouts-rimés*, beginnings and middles of lines, ideas in the rough, like Shelley's scraps, and the least of them so intense, so sweet, so palpitating. . . (*DP*, p. 317).

She feels she is 'sleeping on a poet's lips, immersed in the very essence of him, permeated by his spirit as by an ether' (*DP*, p. 318). In diagnosing the contemporary death of the author, Barthes has noted how in ordinary culture the 'image of literature' is 'tyrannically centred on the author, his person, his life, his tastes, his passions', while the book is 'only a tissue of signs, an imitation that is lost, infinitely deferred'.[22] The reader of such signs, like Ella in her bedroom, is 'without history'; she is, as Barthes phrases it, 'simply that *someone* who holds together in a single field all the traces by which the written text is constituted'.[23] Trewe is indeed the ideal post-structuralist writer, silent and invisible. Writing, Barthes holds, 'is the destruction of every voice, of every point of origin'.[24]

Ella unwillingly returns to provincial life, corresponding with Trewe under her pseudonym, and gradually succumbing to her role as wife and mother. Her revelations about Trewe are virtually disregarded by her (conveniently) boorish husband, and she finally dies in childbirth. Jane Gallop has described how the hysteric's contestation 'is contained and co-opted, and, like any victory of the familiar, the familial over the heterogeneous and alien, this containment serves to strengthen the family'.[25] In Hardy's text the children remain invisible, taken for walks along the beach by the nurse, and making brief appearances to interrupt Ella's reveries. The heroine knows only too much about conception, pregnancy and childbirth, and it is this knowledge which has led her into hysteria. Foucault has remarked that the figure of the mother was the most overt form of the hystericization of women's bodies during the nineteenth century, the cult of motherhood being produced concurrently with the notion of the hysterical woman: the mother, he writes, 'with her negative image of "nervous woman", constituted the most visible form of this hysterisation'.[26] Ella stands in a triangular relationship which enables her to mediate between two types of masculinity, the businessman and the poet. As a mother, the story finds her wanting; she reflects 'how wicked she was, a woman having a husband and three children, to let her mind stray to a stranger in this unconscionable manner' (*DP*, p. 317). Her fantasy life is devoted to one object, an encounter with Trewe. Donning his mantle, adopting a male pseudonym, she seeks to deny her 'feminity'; her productions, whether children or poems, are rejected as worthless evidence of Ella's struggle to give birth to herself. The verses she writes (never reproduced for the reader) are part and parcel of her unavailing struggle for meaning, a struggle which is both articulated against, and in conformity with, male dominance.

In projecting the 'sad act' (*DP*, p. 325) of Trewe's suicide, Hardy's tale retains its strange congruence with biography. In 'An Imaginative Woman' the author endorses and denigrates Florence Henniker's literary creativity while simultaneously proclaiming his own artistic mastery and imagining an oblivion brought about by her failure to respond to his advances. The literal death of the author in the tale conforms with uncanny accuracy to Kristeva's definition of the artist as,

> melancholy's most intimate witness and the most ferocious combatant of the symbolic abdication enveloping him—until death strikes and suicide imposes its triumphant conclusion upon the void of the lost object.[27]

The 'lost object' in this case is that very 'female friend', 'tenderly devoted to me', whom Trewe has dreamt of; the 'undiscoverable, elusive one' who remains 'unrevealed, unmet, unwon' (*DP*, p. 325), and who, within the multiplying ironies of the tale, now reads Trewe's final confessional letter. Removing himself from the scene where he was a shadowy absence, the poet endorses the Foucauldian analysis of the way writing 'has become linked to sacrifice, even to the sacrifice of life'. In this process of 'voluntary effacement', and in the creation of the narrative which frames it, the work of art which once, in Foucault's phrase, 'had the duty of providing immortality', 'now

possesses the right to kill, to be its author's murderer'.[28] The intimate
relationship between death and writing, always hinted at in the
tremulous entwining of Trewe and his shadow, 'John Ivy', becomes
dramatically manifest in 'the effacement of the writing subject's individual characteristics'.[29] Indeed, Foucault's general critique is borne
out within the economy of Hardy's tale: 'the mark of the writer is
reduced to nothing more than the singularity of his absence'. Trapped
within his role, and unknowingly feeding off the hapless Ella, Trewe
must therefore finally assume 'the role of the dead man in the game of
writing'.[30] The fluidity and continuity of writing halts in Trewe's final
act. It is through the 'conscious death' of suicide, Mikhail Bakhtin
claims, that those links are forged 'in the conscious chain where a man
finalises himself from within'.[31]

3. *'Barbara of the House of Grebe'*

'Barbara of the House of Grebe' (1890–91) stands as a crux in Hardy's
work. T.S. Eliot spoke disparagingly of its inhabiting a 'world of pure
Evil',[32] and Bayley has complained that the story is 'notably lacking in
any of the real pleasures' of Hardy's texts.[33] Certainly the subdued
erotic violence of the tale feels disturbing, but it is to some extent held
and distanced by the voice of the narrator, an elderly surgeon who
recounts the narrative as one which has been recovered from local
history and gossip.

It is, on the surface, a story easily told. Barbara, the daughter of Sir
John and Lady Grebe, falls in love with a young man called Edmond
Willowes, a handsome youth of humble background. She is being
courted by the impassive Lord Uplandtowers, and the aristocrat's
unwanted attentions lead the young couple to elope. The Grebes
become reconciled to the *mésalliance*, and Willowes is sent on a Grand
Tour to acquire some social graces. His heroic action at a theatre fire
in Venice results in terrible facial disfigurement. Willowes returns to
England, but Barbara is repulsed by his appearance. By the time she
experiences a change of heart, her husband has left. He disappears,
and it is later disclosed that he has died on the continent. Lord
Uplandtowers, her frigidly persistent admirer, returns to court her
and she finally marries him. The marriage is unhappy, Uplandtowers
blaming Barbara both for her lack of affection and for her failure to
produce an heir to the estate. When a lifesize statue of Willowes

arrives from Italy, she begins secretly to worship it at night. Lord Uplandtowers arranges for a craftsman to disfigure the statue so that it resembles the injured man, and at the sight of this mutilation Barbara is struck dumb. When her husband places the statue at the end of the marital bed, his wife becomes epileptic. Barbara is now reduced to an attitude of passionate servility towards her second husband. She later gives birth to ten children, only one of whom survives into adulthood, and finally dies abroad.

The framing device of the stories gathered together as *A Group of Noble Dames* is that of a number of different narrators recounting tales of Wessex aristocratic women at a dinner party. There is, therefore, an unsophisticated general narration which is to be understood in the reading of each individual tale, a device which draws attention to the literariness of each story while also subverting any inside/outside polarity. Indeed, Hardy was at pains to defend the Gothic elements of 'Barbara of the House of Grebe' by pointing out how the action is cast 'into a second plane or middle distance, being described by a character to characters, and not point-blank by author to reader'.[34] The framed tale serves to dialogize the speech of the narrator through the silent presence of the narratees who act as surrogates for the reader. The story of Barbara thus regresses into previous writings, Dorset family history and local memory so that the origins of the tale do not lie with the narrator, but are scattered traces to which he gives a temporary voice. In fact, at some points the narrator takes credit for his own uncertainties, describing Barbara's appearance on her return from the elopement, for example, 'according to the tale handed down by old women' (*DP*, p. 218), claiming that Willowes's farewell note was 'something like' what he transcribes (*DP*, p. 229), and recalling how in childhood he 'knew an old lady whose mother saw the wedding' between Barbara and Uplandtowers (*DP*, p. 232).

However it wishes to be read, 'Barbara of the House of Grebe' communicates a fundamental obsession with the non-attainment of sexual goals. At its centre, the Pygmalion-like episode of the statue suggests that an ideal aesthetic image is preferred to a living body, or to the quotidian banality of sexual intercourse:

> The statue was a full-length figure, in the purest Carrara marble, representing Edmond Willowes in all his original beauty, as he had stood at parting from her when about to set out on his travels; a specimen of manhood almost perfect in every line and contour. The work had been carried out with absolute fidelity (*DP*, p. 233).

Barbara stands 'in a sort of trance', 'lost in reverie' before what Lord
Uplandtowers designates 'the monstrous thing' (*DP*, p. 234). The man
she was unable to love in life inspires endless devotion through his
transfiguration into timeless image, and it is this metamorphosis which
ironically undercuts the Dean of Melchester's closing homily on 'the
folly of indulgence in sensuous love for a handsome form merely'
(*DP*, p. 243). The cleric is only the first of the tale's misreaders. The
story plays with and upon the relationship between art, literature and
sexuality in its handling of a pleasurable deferral of consummation
which may take Browning's 'The Statue and the Bust' as its intertext.
The statue triggers off a desire which can never be fulfilled, mirror-
ing the movement of postponement implicit in the act of reading the
text. The function of the statue is not simply to reduplicate Willowes's
appearance (the willowy flexuousness of his body transmuted into the
stillness of marble), but also to reverse the sexual roles so that the
female becomes agent and instigator.

Both males acquire the same stolid fixity, the phlegmatic phallic
imperviosity of the aristocrat being paradoxically transferred to his
young rival in the reification emblematized in the statue, and against
the note of male implacability the tale schematically places the female,
represented as timid, emotional and finally hysterical. Division and
non-merging create the narrative *frisson* which reaches its height in
the disfigurement of Willowes, which in a curious pattern of repetition is then applied to the statue. As the accompanying tutor reveals to
Lord Uplandtowers, Willowes escaped from the fire with ' "Neither
nose nor ears, nor lips scarcely" ' (*DP*, p. 237), and it is upon this
symbolic castration and cancellation of the marks of difference that
the meaning of the tale depends. In *Totem and Taboo* Freud noted
how, in tribal rituals, 'One of the most widespread magic procedures
for injuring an enemy consists of making an effigy of him out of any
kind of material'.[35] Hardy's chronology reverses the anthropological
pattern whereby, as Freud observes, 'whatever is subsequently done to
this image will also happen to the hated prototype'.[36] The stress upon
the power of suggestion here is strangely parallel to Hardy's tale.
Elsewhere, Freud was to argue that the value of transference in analysis is that it is not simply a repetition of past real erotic impulses:
'when all is said and done, it is impossible to destroy anyone *in absen-
tia* or *in effigie*'.[37]

'Barbara of the House of Grebe' is disturbing because it deals with
transgression, and imagines human sexuality as a drive which creates

division and postponement. The aim of the narrative is to upset and
overturn readerly expectations through its juggling with stereotypical
characters. Willowes is presented quite externally as the innocent,
energetic, manly hero, and Uplandtowers as his pallid and cold-
hearted rival, while Barbara is caught in the trajectory between the
two in her irresolute behaviour patterns. Yet the fate of the two men
is markedly opposite to expectations: Willowes, handsome and lively,
is exiled, disfigured, ostracized and reduced to immobility; Uplandtowers, calculatingly cynical in his 'doggedness' (*DP*, p. 211), acts
with vengeful energy at the crisis. It is as if, in these late stories, the
representative stability of nineteenth-century character-drawing is
abruptly and laconically challenged by opposing modes of reading;
Willowes's simplicity and legibility of character stands in contradistinction to the opaque impassivity of Uplandtowers. Willowes thus
doubles for the writer as mimetic realist, his statue, notably, a work
'carried out with absolute fidelity' to its model (*DP*, p. 233), while his
lordship embodies an ironized, modernist form of reading. De Man
has argued that the modernist assertion of the superiority of reading
over writing 'reflects the shift in the concept of text from an imitative
to a hermeneutic model'. Meaning which is, like Willowes's statue,
'openly asserted and visible' in the imitative text, becomes 'concealed'
and 'has to be disclosed by a labour of decoding and interpretation' in
the modern hermeneutic text. The distinction between the open visage
of the hero prior to disfigurement (echoed in the statue) and the veiled
impenetrability of Uplandtowers enacts a distinction which de Man
traces between 'intended and stated meaning that it is in the author's
interest to keep hidden'. Hardy's schematic characterization of the two
men registers his creative vacillation between different modes of
writing and reading. Indeed, the difference between the two marks
nothing less than 'the mastery of the writer over his text', a mastery
dependent upon 'the bewilderment and confusion of [the] reader', as
de Man puts it. The status of the reader's performance, in such a text,
will remain 'perilously poised' between something which is 'a simulacrum', like the statue, and what de Man terms 'the real thing'.[38] The
donning of the mask by the disfigured hero is a sign of his entering
the more complex world of representation, an opening up of the gap
between signified and signifier which earlier he has elided in the naive
simplicity of his being. The mask hides, erases and stresses the marks
of difference in his damaged physiognomy, while Lord Uplandtowers's
violent reaction to the statue suggests a hidden complicity with the

Adonis-figure of the hero. Indeed the peer's evil behaviour suggests a covert connection between the two readings of life, and provides a provocative paradigm of the reader's activity as she simultaneously creates and consumingly destroys the text. In the scene of the disfigured statue Lord Uplandtowers acts almost as Barbara's analyst, placing himself in a position of male mastery and control. The statue 'belongs' to Barbara as a substitute, such an analyst might suggest, for the phallus she does not possess; it fits into the 'alcove' in her boudoir but is also veiled and concealed by the cupboard she builds to house it.[39] The clandestine female worship of the statue accords with powerful male fantasies of display and concealment, and his lordship's mutilation of the marble suggests an aggressive investment in the castration complex. The tableau of Barbara worshipping at the shrine of Willowes's statue, voyeuristically spied upon by her second husband, takes the form of a primal scene of considerable power:

> Arrived at the door of the boudoir, he beheld the door of the private recess open, and Barbara within it, standing with her arms clasped tightly round the neck of her Edmond, and her mouth on his. The shawl which she had thrown round her nightclothes had slipped from her shoulders, and her long white robe and pale face lent her the blanched appearance of a second statue embracing the first. Between her kisses, she apostrophised it in a low murmur of infantine tenderness:
> 'My only love—how could I be so cruel to you, my perfect one—so good and true—I am ever faithful to you, despite my seeming infidelity! I always think of you—dream of you—during the long hours of the day, and in the night-watches! O Edmond, I am always yours!' Such words as these, intermingled with sobs, and streaming tears, and dishevelled hair, testified to an intensity of feeling in his wife which Lord Uplandtowers had not dreamed of her possessing (*DP*, p. 236).

The implications of this scene are, literally, excessive: the image of Barbara feeds upon both the Gothic stereotype of the crazed woman and the Victorian categorization of female hysteria. Her eyes are at the centre of a spectacle which is met in turn by the controlling gaze of the male. Uplandtowers is, as it were, watching an act of sexual intercourse between Willowes and Barbara. Indeed, the landowner seems to be attempting to reconstitute a type of primal scene in which he plays the roles of witness/voyeur. He wishes to see the woman's sexual abandon, while the narrator/reader curiously occupies the positions of observer and observed, such is the recalcitrant instability of the text at this juncture. Through this act of seeing, Lord

Uplandtowers seeks to supplant Willowes. He wishes both to denounce his rival and to remain hidden, and his eccentric method leads him into a parodic type of aversion therapy; he repeats the 'grisly exhibition' of the mutilated statue several times, 'Firm in enforcing his ferocious correctives' in a systematic application of what the narrator oddly phrases 'virtuous tortures' (*DP*, p. 240). In the writing of such a scene, Hardy uncannily corroborates Benjamin's brilliant diagnosis of the Proustian treatment of lesbianism:

> [Proust] in a certain fashion ventures into the tidy private chamber within the petit bourgeois that bears the inscription *sadism* and then mercilessly smashes everything to pieces, so that nothing remains of the untarnished, clear-cut conception of wickedness, but instead within every fracture evil explicitly shows its true substance—'humanity', or even 'kindness'.[40]

Uplandtowers is possessed of all the strength and willpower which Barbara patently lacks, and in one sense the scene might be construed as a scene of the errant daughter's seduction; the monumental rigour of male rationality, in seeking to control and contain female hysteria, reveals itself as an effect of what it excludes. Barbara's identity is formed purely within the terms of her relations with men. She is less a speaking subject than an object of enunciation. In clasping the statue, she takes on 'the blanched appearance of a second statue embracing the first' (*DP*, p. 236). Jacqueline Rose has noted how Freud's work on hysteria began with the rejection of Charcot's theory of bodily hysteric zones:

> By so doing he made of hysteria a language (made it speak) but one whose relation to the body was decentered, since if the body spoke it was precisely because there was something called the unconscious that could not.[41]

Rose argues against any notion of female sexuality as content or substance, preferring to emphasize 'a concept of sexuality as caught up in the register of demand and desire'. Sexual difference is culturally constructed at a price, involving 'subjection to a law which exceeds any natural or biological division'. The concept of the phallus, represented here by the statue, 'stands for that subjection, and for the way in which women are very precisely implicated in its process'.[42] Barbara is, throughout the tale, caught up in, and defined by, a web of male discourse and perception. The hysteric subject refuses the ordering inherent in 'normal' sexuality; this is the origin of the hysteric's symptoms, which arise out of an apparent lack of continuity between disordered behaviour and the normalizing force of human speech. In gazing spellbound at the statue, Barbara allows herself to become an object of control. Indeed, her actions are significantly parallel in a number of ways to those of Charcot's female patients at the Salpêtrière in Paris. As Elaine Showalter observes, Charcot's lectures were remarkably dependent upon the use of visual aids (including statues); while based upon close observation of his patients, Charcot's treatment paid 'very little attention to what they were saying'.[43] Lord Uplandtowers significantly ignores Barbara's pleas to have the statue removed from the marital bedroom, until she is reduced to an epileptic silence:

> The third night, when the scene had opened as usual, and she lay staring with immense wild eyes at the horrid fascination, on a sudden she gave an unnatural laugh; she laughed more and more, staring at the image, till she literally shrieked with laughter: then there was silence, and he found her to have become insensible. He thought she had fainted, but soon saw that the event was worse: she was in an epileptic fit (*DP*, p. 240).

Showalter reflects that, in the late nineteenth century, 'hysteria was at best a private, ineffectual response to the frustrations of women's lives', and the 'gratifications' of the condition were 'slight in relation to its costs in powerlessness and silence'.[44] The emotional content of these scenes is complex in its overlapping of fear, spectacle and the ludicrous. It is, clearly, the woman's role to be inspected and studied in the throes of a sexual passion which threatens male hegemony, and this potent fantasy of erotic surveillance would seem to have its roots deep in Hardy's psyche. In the course of describing Hardy's youthful fascination with hangings, and notably with the execution of a young woman at Dorchester, Robert Gittings remarks upon 'an early thread of perverse morbidity in Hardy, something near abnormality',[45] and it may be this aspect of the story which led Eliot to claim that it was written 'solely to provide a satisfaction for some morbid emotion'.[46] The authorial gaze blends into the masterful look of Uplandtowers in a scene which both re-enacts the exercise of psychic mastery at the Salpêtrière and displays the making of the modern soul through those methods of 'punishment, supervision and constraint' which Foucault examines in *Discipline and Punish*.[47] The triangular structure of spying husband, hysterical wife and statue gains something of its *frisson* from what Foucault, speaking of the unitary power of the gaze in the Benthamite panopticon, characterizes as 'a certain concerted distribution of bodies, surfaces, lights, gazes'. The motivation of the watcher in this Foucauldian scene is of little import, and Uplandtowers's motivation appears to be an uneasy blend of 'the curiosity of the indiscreet, the malice of a child, the thirst for knowledge of a philosopher. . . or the perversity of those who take pleasure in spying and punishing'.[48]

There is also an undertow of class feeling to be remarked on in these scenes, Lord Uplandtowers's aristocratic resentment against his social inferiors spilling over into the severity with which he treats both the statue and the 'poachers, smugglers, and turnip-stealers' (*DP*, p. 231) who come before him on the bench. Class and gender relations equally mirror an exploitative economic system, and the statue scene leads inevitably to the taming of Barbara's sexuality in the name of eugenics. When, earlier, there has been no sign of an heir, his lordship brusquely demands of Barbara 'what she was good for' (*DP*, p. 232). She is tamed, at the end of the tale, to a 'servile mood of attachment', a 'cure' which, in reducing his wife to an over-attentive slave, strikes Uplandtowers as nothing less than 'a new disease' (*DP*, p. 241). While Barbara ends her life in 'obsequious amativeness towards a perverse and cruel man' (*DP*, p. 242), it is hard to perceive greater tragedy here than in her earlier life. Her first marriage is characterized by the permanent absence of her husband and by her immurement in the dismally solitary Yewsholt Lodge which her 'kind-hearted father' (*DP*, p. 220) makes over to her; her second marriage is a continuous exposure to sadism and blocked emotion. The crucial disturbance registered in the statue scene goes hand in hand with a coolly voyeuristic quality in the narrative voice itself, a voice irresolutely balanced between sympathy for, and denigration of, the heroine. There is a covert enjoyment of the 'quick spasm of horror' (*DP*, p. 227) when Barbara sees Willowes unmasked, of the 'loud and prolonged shriek' (*DP*, p. 238) which resounds when she sees the damaged statue, and the 'low scream' (*DP*, p. 240) she emits when the statue is revealed at the end of the marital bed. The almost diabolic reappearances of Lord Uplandtowers—while Barbara walks alone at Yewsholt Lodge, as she awaits the return of Willowes at Lornton Inn, and finally after Willowes's second departure—act out an animus within the narrative itself which forces the unfortunate heroine first into misplaced philanthropy and finally into the 'reserved beatification' (*DP*, p. 234) of her dead lover. A kind of narratorial panic about the nature of female sexual identity structures the story as a repeated series of scenes of punishment and entrapment neatly epitomized in the scene where Barbara, fleeing from the sight of her husband's damaged face, seeks refuge for the night in a greenhouse:

> Here she remained, her great timid eyes strained through the glass upon the garden without, and her skirts gathered up, in fear of the field-mice which sometimes came there. Every moment she dreaded to hear footsteps which she ought by law to have longed for, and a voice that should have been as music to her soul (*DP*, p. 228).

The childish fear of the mice is added to the fear of the man's footsteps in a curious act of narrative malignity, the whole framed by the reverberations of that male 'law' to which the heroine throughout is required to submit. It is as though, in 'Barbara of the House of Grebe', the form of the narrative itself is troubled by the phenomenon of female desire, and this trouble leads the author into a powerfully undecidable oscillation between sympathy and scorn.

The spectacular scene of the statue concentrates this complex of feelings, registering a fear of narrative flow and openness in the desire for the fixity and closure imaged in the marble figure. Maurice Blanchot remarks upon the inability of the artist to 'put an end' to his work until circumstances, 'in the form of the publisher, financial obligations, social requirements—put an arbitrary end to this endlessness'. The statue, in its immobile potency, imposes such formal closure in Hardy's narrative. Indeed, Blanchot appropriately goes on to observe,

> if the statue is a glorification of marble, and if all art tends towards an elucidation of the primal depth which the world negates and rejects so that it can assert itself, has not the language of poetry and literature the same relation to ordinary language as the image has to the object?[49]

It is not necessary to recruit Hardy to the decadent movement to perceive the vengeful attack upon the statue as a revelation, in the work's unconscious, of a wished-for valorization and simultaneous repudiation of literature and authority upon Hardy's part. Willowes is no Dorian Gray, but the aesthetic form of his statue, and its destruction, plays upon similar artistic and sexual notions. Willowes, as it were, steps out of life into art, but the literary language of this tale is inextricably linked with a troubling sexuality, or perhaps an absence of sexuality which is even more disturbing. The genital 'deep recess' (*DP*, p. 234) into which the statue is inserted suggests both male otherness and the confirmation of Barbara's necessarily secretive femininity.

The stilling of body, life and action into statue hints at the cost of art, the way the life-force of the artist is conceived, in both romantic and modernist mythology, as draining away into the aesthetic object.[50] Eliot's dictum, in 'Tradition and the Individual Talent', that the 'progress of an artist' consists in 'a continual extinction of personality',[51] nicely mirrors this tale in which the obsessively private Hardy imaginatively inhabits first the mask and then the statue. The translation of Willowes from human being to statue may be illuminated by Derrida's concern for the 'dangerous' qualities of transcription:

> dangerous, not because it refers to writing, but because it presupposes a text which would be already there, immobile: the serene presence of a statue, of a written stone or archive whose signified content might be harmlessly transported into the milieu of a different language, that of the preconscious or the conscious.[52]

The death of Willowes, emblematized in the marmoreal image of the statue, closes off the possibility of relationship or growth for Barbara, just as it enforces closure upon the structure of the tale. The act of writing and the free play of signification here run up against what Derrida characterizes as a 'fundamental ground', or a 'play constituted on the basis of a fundamental immobility and a reassuring certitude, which itself is beyond the reach of play'. Only through such apparent certitude may anxiety be mastered in the myth of a 'full presence which is beyond play'.[53] The statue, a final presence created out of an absence, imposes an effect of closure only through the 'finality' of death, and the attack upon it reads like a covert attack upon the literary artefact; it is as if Hardy were a party to that 'pure murder of literature' which Barthes identifies as 'the torment and the justification of the modern writer'.[54] Indeed the disfiguration of the statue might well draw upon opposing models of literary form to make its full impact upon the reader: the classicism which insists on normative rules and unified texts is exposed to murderous attack by a romanticism which values fragmentation above all. 'Barbara of the House of Grebe' demands to be read as something more and also something less than a parodic Gothic tale; as Hardy's handling of the genre gains in sophistication it also grows increasingly explicit, erupting into the breathtaking naivety of the statue scenes. Foucault has identified Gothic as a genre which has peculiarly always contained parodic elements. Gothic tales, he argues, 'are accompanied by an ironic movement which doubles and divides them':

> It is as if two twin and complementary languages were born at once from the same central source; one existing entirely in its naivety, the other within parody; one existing solely for the reader's eyes, the other moving from the readers' simple-minded fascination to the easy tricks of the writer. But in actuality, these two languages are more than simply contemporaneous; they lie within each other, share the same dwelling, constantly intertwine, forming a single verbal web and, as it were, a forked language that turns against itself from within, destroying itself in its own body, poisonous in its very density.[55]

Such a doubling of language is enabling and disabling within Hardy's text, the rhetoric of persuasive horror mingling irresistibly with an extremity of absurdism. As Willowes's face is reduced to a featureless mass, so the narrative itself turns increasingly blank; it is this absence of feature which has prompted the critical debate surrounding the story.

The statue occupies a space which is empty; it is a sign both replete with and innocent of meaning, neither masculine nor feminine, challenging the limits of sexual division through its smooth homogeneity. Willowes's bodily grace is concentrated in his facial beauty. He is, remarks the narrator, 'one of the handsomest men who ever set his lips on a maid's' (*DP*, p. 218). This quality takes on a crucial signifying role within the narrative. The face, Derrida suggests, has functioned in the Western tradition as 'the original unity of glance and speech, eyes and mouth'. As such, the face does not signify anything other than 'self, soul, subjectivity'. The human face represents a primordial 'unthinkable unity' of speech which exists in violent opposition to writing: 'Thought is speech, and is therefore immediately face'. The face is 'not a metaphor, not a figure', while writing is wholly constituted through, and undermined by, figuration. Derrida discerns the recognition of a radical alterity in the face, and an 'irreducible violence' in the necessity of discourse formed through the recognition of the 'other', 'an appearing which dissimulates its essential dissimulation, takes it out of the light, stripping it, and hiding that which is hidden in the other'. Discourse arises out of difference, and is always turned 'against itself'. The naked ego represents 'the absolute form of experience', an absolute always already invaded by alterity and the violent necessity of discourse.[56] Willowes, in the innocent homogeneity of his sameness, is thus subject to the violent discourse through which Uplandtowers asserts the identity of the other, the duplicitous exigencies of language and the supremacy of the land-owning class.

What happens in Hardy's tale is the progressive obliteration of the face, first behind the mask which Willowes dons to hide his (missing) features, then in the disfigurement carried out at the behest of Lord Uplandtowers. The moment of recognition of the mask marks a crisis of misrecognition in the text:

> When he came forward into the light of the lamp, she perceived with surprise, and almost with fright, that he wore a mask. At first she had not noticed this—there being nothing in its colour which would lead a casual observer to think he was looking on anything but a real countenance (*DP*, p. 225).

Barbara realizes that Willowes's voice is both different and the same; his tones 'were not unlike the old tones', but 'the enunciation was so altered as to seem that of a stranger' (*DP*, p. 225). The unified subject, represented in the romantically pure features of the hero, is revealed as fundamentally split and decentered, the claim to identity and selfhood compromised by its dependence upon strategies of disguise and concealment. In his analysis of voice and mask, de Man describes how, in Greek tragedy, the wearing of the mask indicated that the voice which spoke was already dead but also lived on. Prosopopeia is the rhetorical figure for this masking of the voice, or voicing of the mask. As de Man argues, voice 'assumes mouth, eye, and finally face',[57] features spectacularly absent in the case of Edmond Willowes. Prosopopeia is especially related to the autobiographical strain in writing, de Man argues, a strain which deals with 'the giving and taking away of faces, with face and deface, *figure*, figuration and disfiguration',[58] but its ambiguous status is revealingly traced in an examination of Wordsworth's *Essays upon Epitaphs*. Wordsworth quotes from Milton's sonnet on Shakespeare:

> Then thou our fancy of itself bereaving
> Dost make us Marble with too much conceiving;

De Man detects here the 'latent threat' in prosopopeia: 'that by making the dead speak, the symmetrical structure of the trope implies, by the same token, that the living are struck dumb, frozen in their own death'.[59] The fragmentation and mutilation of the statue uncannily doubles the kind of self-mutilation involved in Hardy's renunciation of his career as a novelist. Such abnegation, although ostensibly undertaken to enable a new career as poet, is a kind of disfigurement. In his discussion of the fragmentary nature of Shelley's *The Triumph of Life*, de Man takes Hardy's tale as a touchstone which allows him to pose the question, 'Is the status of a text like the status of a statue?'[60] The writer, like both the protagonist in the Hardy tale and the author, moves from 'erased self-knowledge to disfiguration'; he 'gains shape, face, or figure only to lose it as he acquires it'.[61] That loss, de Man holds, is marked by the violence of that element in thought 'that destroys thought in its attempt to forget its duplicity'. Such 'repetitive erasures' may aptly enough be designated 'disfiguration'.[62] Willowes, the epitome of beauty, inevitably is subject to the loss of the contours of his face. The mutilated text of *The Triumph of Life*, permanently interrupted by Shelley's drowning, becomes paradigmatic here, exposing the 'wound of a fracture that lies hidden in all texts'.[63] This wound can only be dressed, as it were, by the reader. Transformation into aesthetic object constitutes a pervasive strategy which the act of reading simultaneously adopts and denies. As Benjamin aphoristically observes, 'The work is the deathmask of its conception'.[64] To read, de Man remarks, 'is to understand, to question, to know, to forget, to erase, to deface, to repeat—that is to say, the endless prosopopeia by which the dead are made to have a face and a voice which tells the allegory of their demise and allows us to apostrophise them in our turn'.[65] The reader of 'Barbara of the House of Grebe' encounters a text at once transparent and legible, like the hero's boyish physiognomy, and bafflingly indecipherable and erased, like his masked visage. Indeed, Willowes's progressive disappearance is best accounted for by Barthes's observations about the irreversibility of speech. Since, as Barthes shows, 'a word cannot be *retracted*', through the operation of a paradox which encompasses the fate of Hardy's protagonist in this text, 'it is ephemeral speech which is indelible', rather than what Barthes characterizes 'monumental writing'.[66] Willowes doubles for the reader in his inextricably linked roles of boyish innocent and masked dissimulator. His relations with death parallel those of the narrator with his text: just as the hero progressively disappears, so the writer is effaced into the mask of a variously decipherable textuality. In Hardy's poem, 'The Masked Face', the speaker, finding himself in a 'giddying place,/With no firm fixéd floor', is informed by a 'mask-clad face' that he has arrived in the realm of human life. As signifier detaches from signified, text becomes site without foundations, in which vertiginous possibilities of reading are opened up. The poem goes on, significantly, to sound the characteristic Hardyan theme of the incomprehensibility of existence through the metaphor of writing:

> The mask put on a bleak smile then,
>   And said, 'O vassal-wight,
> There once complained a goosequill pen
>   To the scribe of the Infinite
>   Of the works it had to write
> Because they were past its ken' (*CP*, p. 522).

The problems of reading 'Barbara of the House of Grebe' stem from the unreadability of the three participants who appear to act out their drama in a limbo removed from any recognizable social or historical context. The conception of the tale owed something to the story of the wife of the fifth Earl of Shaftesbury, as recounted in John Hutchins's eighteenth-century compilation of the history of Dorset, a work closely studied by Hardy in its mid-Victorian third edition. But the oral tradition was also crucial. Hardy claimed that he had drawn, in composing *A Group of Noble Dames*, upon 'some legendary notes I had taken down from the lips of aged people in a remote part of the country, where traditions of the local families linger on, and are remembered by the yeomen and peasantry long after they are forgotten by the families concerned'.[67] It is precisely the absence of these remembrancers, the Wessex craftsmen and workfolk, which inserts the actors of 'Barbara of the House of Grebe' into a troubling vacuum. The structures of ownership and production, of work and social relations, are invisible here as they are not, for example, in *The Woodlanders* or *Tess of the d'Urbervilles*. This is not to argue that such texts mediate or express a historical reality. As George Wotton has put it, Hardy's writing is 'situated in relation to a definable historical process', while it is 'not rooted directly in historical reality'. 'Another reality', he argues, 'mediates the relation between history and writing, the reality of ideology'.[68] The family seats of the two aristocratic families are carefully described at the outset of the story. While it is stressed that the Grebe baronetcy owns lands 'even more extensive' and 'well-enclosed' than those of the earl (*DP*, p. 212), the possession of land and title, and the dispossession of the common people, remains a blind spot within the melodrama of the narrative. The working population of Wessex are literally invisible to the text and its readership. As Wotton remarks, there exists 'no identity between what Hardy wanted the reader to "see" and the image of the ideological produced by Hardy's writing'.[69] What Raymond Williams classically identified as Hardy's centrality, his sense of tension 'between customary and educated feeling and thought',[70] is a defining absence in this story, where sadism and hysteria coexist with a textuality whose pleasurable dangers are produced through an irrevocable divorce from history. It was that divorce, ultimately, which led to Hardy's abandonment of fiction in favour of the private voice of the poet.

Notes

1. K. Brady, *The Short Stories of Thomas Hardy* (London: Macmillan, 1982), pp. 95, 97, 121, 124.

2. J. Hillis Miller, 'Thomas Hardy, Jacques Derrida, and the "Dislocation of Souls"', in *Taking Chances: Derrida, Psychoanalysis and Literature* (ed. J. Smith and W. Kerrigan; Baltimore: Johns Hopkins University Press, 1984), p. 135.

3. Hillis Miller, '"Dislocation"', p. 136.

4. Hillis Miller, '"Dislocation"', p. 136.

5. Hillis Miller, '"Dislocation"', p. 137. It is not the least of the 'little ironies' disclosed here that Henry Fielding, arch-parodist of the epistolary form, had practised as a barrister on the western circuit in the early 1740s.

6. T. Docherty, *On Modern Authority* (Brighton: Harvester, 1987), p. 214.

7. Docherty, *Authority*, p. 214.

8. P. Stallybrass and A. White, *The Politics and Poetics of Transgression* (London: Methuen, 1986), p. 178.

9. Stallybrass and White, *Transgression*, p. 180.

10. Stallybrass and White, *Transgression*, pp. 182-83.

11. Stallybrass and White, *Transgression*, p. 187.

12. Benjamin, *Charles Baudelaire*, p. 130.

13. Millgate, *Thomas Hardy*, p. 342.

14. Millgate, *Thomas Hardy*, p. 342.

15. J. Derrida, *Writing and Difference* (trans. A. Bass; London: Routledge & Kegan Paul, 1978), pp. 205-11.

16. Derrida, *Writing and Difference*, p. 197.

17. Gallop, *Feminism and Psychoanalysis*, p. 74.

18. Gallop, *Feminism and Psychoanalysis*, p. 75.

19. Gallop, *Feminism and Psychoanalysis*, p. 66.

20. Sigmund Freud, 'Three Essays on Sexuality', in *On Sexuality*, p. 91.

21. E. Showalter, *The Female Malady* (London: Virago, 1987), p. 147.

22. Barthes, *Image, Music, Text*, pp. 143, 147.

23. Barthes, *Image, Music, Text*, p. 148.

24. Barthes, *Image, Music, Text*, p. 142.

25. Gallop, *Feminism and Psychoanalysis*, p. 133.

26. M. Foucault, *The History of Sexuality*, I (trans. R. Hurley; Harmondsworth: Penguin Books, 1981), p. 104.

27. J. Kristeva, 'On the Melancholic Imaginary', in *Discourse in Psychoanalysis and Literature* (ed. S. Rimmon-Kenan; London: Methuen, 1987), p. 105.

28. M. Foucault, 'What is an Author?', in *The Foucault Reader* (ed. P. Rabinow; Harmondsworth: Penguin Books, 1986), p. 102.

29. Foucault, 'Author?', p. 102.

30. Foucault, 'Author?', pp. 102-103.

31. M.M. Bakhtin, *Problems of Dostoevsky's Poetics* (trans. C. Emerson; Manchester: Manchester University Press, 1988), p. 296.

32. T.S. Eliot, *After Strange Gods* (London: Faber & Faber, 1934), p. 58.

33. Bayley, *Essay on Hardy*, p. 21.

34. Letter of 10 July 1891, cited in Millgate, *Thomas Hardy*, p. 316. Hardy added, 'A good horror has its place in art'.

35. Sigmund Freud, *Totem and Taboo* (trans. A.A. Brill; Harmondsworth: Penguin Books, 1938), p. 112.

36. Freud, *Totem and Taboo*, p. 112.

37. Sigmund Freud, 'The Dynamics of Transference', in *The Standard Edition of the Complete Psychological Works*, XII (trans. J. Strachey; London: Hogarth Press, 1958), p. 108.

38. P. de Man, *The Rhetoric of Romanticism* (New York: Columbia University Press, 1984), pp. 281-82.

39. 'Barbara of the House of Grebe' was one of the stories in *A Group of Noble Dames* which offended the sensibilities of the editor of the *Graphic*, for which they were intended. The assistant editor reminded Hardy that the Victorian *paterfamilias* would not approve 'a series of tales almost every one of which turns upon questions of childbirth, and those relations between the sexes over which conventionality is accustomed. . . to draw a veil' (cited in Millgate, *Thomas Hardy*, p. 305).

40. Walter Benjamin, *Moscow Diary* (ed. G. Smith; trans R. Sieburth; Cambridge, MA: Harvard University Press, 1986), pp. 94-95.

41. Rose, *Sexuality*, p. 38.

42. *Sexuality*, pp. 47, 51.

43. Showalter, *Female Malady*, p. 154.

44. Showalter, *Female Malady*, p. 161.

45. R. Gittings, *Young Thomas Hardy* (Harmondsworth: Penguin Books, 1978), p. 61.

46. Eliot, *After Strange Gods*, p. 58.

47. M. Foucault, *Discipline and Punish* (trans. A. Sheridan; Harmondsworth: Penguin Books, 1979), p. 29.

48. Foucault, *Discipline and Punish*, p. 202.

49. M. Blanchot, *The Sirens' Song* (ed. G. Josipovici; trans. S. Rabinovitch; Brighton: Harvester, 1982), pp. 97, 108.

50. This problem is classically treated within the period in a number of Ibsen's plays. In *When We Dead Awaken* (1899), for instance, Rubek achieved fame through the 'dead figure' of his statue of Irene, who wishes she had 'smashed it to

pieces' before they separated. It was at a performance of *The Master Builder* in 1893 that Hardy found an opportunity to declare his feelings to Florence Henniker, a declaration 'received with distinct coolness' (Millgate, *Thomas Hardy*, p. 337).

51. T.S. Eliot, *Selected Prose* (ed. J. Hayward; Harmondsworth: Penguin Books, 1953), p. 26.

52. Derrida, *Writing and Difference*, p. 211.

53. Derrida, *Writing and Difference*, p. 279.

54. R. Barthes, 'Baudelaire's Theatre', in *A Barthes Reader* (ed. S. Sontag; London: Jonathan Cape, 1982), p. 80. It is of course Barthes, in *S/Z*, who provides the seminal analysis of the relation between statuary, the castration complex and death. Uplandtowers's defacement of the statue uncannily parallels Sarrasine's unsuccessful attack upon his statue of La Zambinella in female form, an attack immediately followed by the sculptor's murder. Hardy was in any case an adept at textual self-mutilation. He was compelled to bowdlerize several of the stories in *A Group of Noble Dames*, including 'Barbara of the House of Grebe', at the instigation of the editors of the *Graphic* prior to serialization. As Simon Gatrell observes, 'When Uplandtowers prepares to mutilate the statue of Willowes, a similar restraint was imposed by the *Graphic*'s editors' (*Hardy the Creator* [Oxford: Clarendon Press, 1988], p. 90). An interesting literary variant is provided in Henri de Régnier's story, 'La Femme de Marbre', first published in 1900.

55. M. Foucault, *Language, Counter-Memory, Practice* (trans. D.F. Bouchard and S. Simon; Ithaca, NY: Cornell University Press, 1977), p. 64.

56. Derrida, *Writing and Difference*, pp. 100, 102, 128, 133.

57. De Man, *Rhetoric of Romanticism*, p. 76.

58. De Man, *Rhetoric of Romanticism*, p. 76.

59. De Man, *Rhetoric of Romanticism*, p. 78.

60. De Man, *Rhetoric of Romanticism*, p. 95.

61. De Man, *Rhetoric of Romanticism*, pp. 100, 103.

62. De Man, *Rhetoric of Romanticism*, pp. 118, 119.

63. De Man, *Rhetoric of Romanticism*, p. 120.

64. Benjamin, *One-Way Street*, p. 65.

65. De Man, *Rhetoric of Romanticism*, p. 122.

66. Barthes, *Image, Music, Text*, p. 190.

67. Letter of 15 July 1891, cited in Millgate, *Thomas Hardy*, p. 317.

68. Wotton, *Thomas Hardy*, p. 73.

69. Wotton, *Thomas Hardy*, p. 88.

70. Williams, *The Country and the City*, p. 198.

PART II

SPEAKING CLASS

Chapter 5

AN INDISCRETION IN THE LIFE OF AN HEIRESS (1878)

The narration of *An Indiscretion in the Life of an Heiress* begins with an eroticized moment of vision which is also a revelation of class difference. The schoolmaster, Egbert Mayne, is attending evening service at Tollamore Church and gazing fixedly at 'one solitary sitter' (*ILH*, p. 29). The youthful heiress of the title, Geraldine Allenville, is sitting beneath a marble monument to her ancestors, a design of 'a winged skull and two cherubim':

> As the youthful schoolmaster gazed, and all these details became dimmer, her face was modified in his fancy, till it seemed almost to resemble the carved marble skull immediately above her head. The thought was unpleasant enough to arouse him from his half-dreamy state, and he entered on rational considerations of what a vast gulf lay between that lady and himself. . . and how painful was the evil when a man of his unequal history was possessed of a keen susceptibility (*ILH*, p. 30).

The story, it is already clear, will centre upon the identification of class division with fantasies of death. Mayne's fraught attempt to cross caste boundaries is charged with a significance which relates problematically to Hardy's own 'story'. Emma Gifford's father, John Attersoll Gifford, had 'greeted his prospective son-in-law with open contempt', and is said to have referred to the young architect as a 'low-born churl who has presumed to marry into *my* family'.[1] Peter Widdowson remarks that, as an author, Hardy inhabited a complex and shifting class position:

> He had strong past and present connections with servants and labourers, with craftsmen more or less thriving, with other more upwardly-mobile relatives, with some of the brutalities and promiscuities of rural social life, with strong elements of autodidacticism, and with people—especially young women—who, by way of education in particular, moved into a different section of the *petit bourgeoisie*.[2]

Thus the commonplace theme of the poor man and the lady takes on a compelling directness in Hardy's imagination, and it may be that the narrator of *An Indiscretion* enacts a kind of literary revenge for the writer's own class humiliation at the hands of the Giffords. This motive lends added piquancy to Patricia Ingham's observation that a significant group of Hardy's protagonists 'perceive themselves as originating on the wrong side of the social divide but are convinced. . . that by delivering a literary text they have crossed it'.[3] Ingham relates the subordinate position of such lower middle-class or working-class figures as Egbert Mayne, Stephen Smith, Swithin St Cleeve or Jude Fawley to the treatment of women in nineteenth-century society. Such subordination, she argues, is fictionally resolved by the introduction of a third sign, that of the artist, and it is the introduction of such a sign—apparently only available to the male protagonist here—which transforms the narrative in the second part of *An Indiscretion*.

Mayne has been first thrown together with Miss Allenville through the introduction of a steam threshing-machine into the local farming community. People gather to look at the new-fangled contraption, among them Geraldine and Egbert, who is related to the farmer who has hired it. Geraldine inadvertently steps back, and is in danger of catching her dress in the machinery and being 'whirled round the wheel as a mangled carcase', when Egbert seizes hold of her and saves her from the engine's toils (*ILH*, pp. 31-32). Within the bourgeois ideology which *An Indiscretion* both endorses and fractures, it becomes inevitable that a type of courtly-love syndrome should follow on from this rescue, Egbert now registering a feeling of 'tender inability to do aught else than defend her against all the world' (*ILH*, p. 33). Thus a dramatic situation is set up which foregrounds its protagonists and reduces the inhabitants of the village, both adult and child, to the role of unwitting minor participants in a romantic *imbroglio*. Sexual desire is felt as isolating in its impact upon the aspirant male, the isolation of the aristocratic female being taken as read. The narrator signals physical attraction through recourse to a journal-istic register of romantic cliché, as when Geraldine visits Egbert at the village school:

> The clear, deep eyes, full of all tender expressions; the fresh, subtly-curved cheek, changing its tones of red with the fluctuation of each thought; the ripe tint of her delicate mouth, and the indefinable line where lip met lip; the noble bend of her neck, the wavy lengths of her dark

brown hair, the soft motions of her bosom when she breathed. . . all
struck him as something he had dreamed of and was not actually seeing
(*ILH*, pp. 35-36).

The routine of the schoolroom is characteristically abandoned in
favour of personal intercourse centring upon the issue of ambition,
and concluding with a reference to the threshing-machine incident.
Egbert, in a symptomatic movement of consciousness, wishes that
Geraldine might betray some awareness 'that he was considerably
more of a man than the small persons by whom the apartment was
mainly filled, and that he was as nearly as possible at her own level in
age, as wide in sympathies, and possibly more inflammable at heart'
(*ILH*, p. 35). The 'few details of routine' are hastily disposed of, and
the rest of the scene is given over to an account of the consciousnesses
of the protagonists. It is a telling moment, and one which Lawrence
would elaborate in Birkin's homily to Ursula in *Women in Love*,
instruction given in the presence of the aristocratic Hermione. In both
scenes the teacher somewhat despises the subject position of the peda-
gogue, and insists that such a public role fails to accord to the 'true'
self. But this mystification cannot obscure the fact that Egbert Mayne
reproduces within his rural classroom the very ideological power
structures from which he suffers, and out of which he seeks to escape.
The text, like its author, is furrowed with self-division in its treatment
of education.

The effects of such a scene are various. Egbert's combative notion
of self-help and Geraldine's patronizing blankness about the realities
of lower-class existence are complicated by the contradictory feeling
of male assertiveness and female receptivity. The characters are
ineluctably caught up within a class system inimical to their desires,
yet this problem is to some extent defused by the blank indeterminacy
of the writing. The schoolroom scenes, and later conversations
between hero and heroine, are fuelled by that 'many-layered and
schizophrenic deception' about class matters which Widdowson detects
in Hardy's disguised autobiography.[4] It is precisely this deception
which depoliticizes the potentially subversive plot of *An Indiscretion*.
The emptying out of political content which produces a pervasive
anonymity of effect may be attributable to the fact that, as Widdowson
argues, 'in the struggle to succeed as man of letters a significant political stance had to be abandoned or suppressed—its vestiges visible only
in the subversive forms and hyper-sensitive class consciousness of the
novels'.[5] The posture of the narrator of *An Indiscretion* is indetermi-

nate, the voice destabilized by the ambiguous freedom and indebted-
ness of Hardy's own class position: 'not of the ruling class, but no
longer, as man of letters, of the lower class and yet still enslaved by
the market and conventional ethics'; such a position necessarily issues
in 'a passive, apolitical alternativism'.[6] The kind of (male) social
ambition proper to a patriarchal society fuels Egbert's later ambition
to become a successful writer, while it is apparently the duty of the
elevated female to remain within the enclosure of her class niche, any
action which compromises this privilege being fraught with danger,
and in this instance leading to death. Geraldine appears as much a
victim as Egbert of the metamorphosis taking place in bourgeois
society. Gender is treated here as a powerful component in the constructed nature of social and personal indentity, and is closely inwoven
with class determinants. In *An Indiscretion*, as in much Hardy fiction,
it is the woman who pays, and this meting out of punishment, as
Widdowson observes, is not attributable simply to a reflectionist
theory of fiction. It is, rather, 'the dominant trajectory of plot and
structure which negates female aspiration'[7]—in this case the subversive aspiration to descend the social ladder—while also unsettling
realist narrative expectations through the typically Hardyan use of
coincidence and symbol. From the beginning of the relationship
Egbert appears to have prescience of Geraldine's demise: in the vision
of her in church her face comes 'almost to resemble the carved
marble skull immediately above her head' (*ILH*, p. 30); she narrowly
escapes death in the steam thresher; and as he watches her leave the
school he reflects 'in rather a melancholy mood how time would
absorb all her beauty' (*ILH*, p. 38). Pathos serves to reduce class
animosity, and thus Geraldine is to be carefully distinguished from
her 'hard-featured' father (*ILH*, p. 65) as a representative of the
appropriating landed class.

The transmutation of landed property into capitalist enterprise
which began with the enclosure acts is explored in the vestigial sub-
plot concerning the tenant farmer Richard Broadford. Broadford,
Egbert's maternal grandfather, is a tenant of Squire Allenville's in a
house which was occupied by his immediate ancestors. However, in a
scheme for enlarging his park, Allenville seeks to dispossess his
tenant. The old man feels he is to be 'swept away' by the proposed
improvements (*ILH*, p. 42). 'The transplanting of old people is like
the transplanting of old trees', the narrator ruminates, 'a twelvemonth
usually sees them wither and die away' (*ILH*, p. 43). Egbert

persuades Geraldine to intercede, and the plan is temporarily put in abeyance. The hero's feelings are now characterized as 'vehement and curious', a contradictory mixture which aptly expresses his class and personal situation:

> Much as he loved her, his liking for the peasantry about him—his mother's ancestry—caused him sometimes a twinge of self-reproach for thinking of her so exclusively, and nearly forgetting his old acquaintance, neighbours, and his grandfather's familiar friends, with their rough but honest ways (*ILH*, p. 49).

A lovers' tiff leads Geraldine to encourage the enlargement of the estate, and although she belatedly repents of this decision, old Broadford, oppressed by the scheme, falls from a corn-stack in the process of threshing and is injured. Before he dies, the old man predicts that the love affair will end badly. As Egbert sits in the house with his uncle's corpse, he is visited by Geraldine and the ice is broken between the two of them. Nevertheless, Egbert reflects that it 'had not crossed her young mind that she was on the verge of committing the most horrible social sin—that of loving beneath her' (*ILH*, p. 62). That 'sin' is nicely registered in the scene of the laying of a foundation stone for a tower which the squire is about to erect 'on the highest hill of his estate, to the memory of his brother, the General' (*ILH*, p. 65). Such a scene emblematically articulates the truths of class difference: at the squire's behest, the entire community is to be dominated and overlooked by a tower which commemorates his family's superiority in the district. The children are to sing, the master-mason and his men to labour, in an act which endorses the role of the Allenvilles as possessors of property. Such a memorializing project is inevitably compromised by the clandestine love affair, but the contaminating effect of class distinction is carefully registered in the conversation of the young couple:

> She glanced round upon the whole landscape stretched out before her, in the extreme distance of which was visible the town of Westcombe.
> 'How long does it take to go to Westcombe across this way?' she asked him while they were bringing up the carriage.
> 'About two hours', he said.
> 'Two hours—so long as that, does it? How far is it away?'
> 'Eight miles.'
> 'Two hours to drive eight miles—who ever heard of such a thing!'
> 'I thought you meant walking.'
> 'Ah, yes; but one hardly means walking without expressly stating it.'

'Well, it seems just the other way to me—that walking is meant unless
you say driving.' (*ILH*, p. 67).

Egbert, who still feels constrained to address Geraldine as 'Madam',
apprises her of his fears about the relationship. Yet the hero is
entirely split, his motivation contradictory. He determines to go to
London to try 'to rise to her level by years of sheer exertion', yet
reflects with a feeble 'rebelliousness' upon the anomaly which compels
him to such a career (*ILH*, p. 73). As Ingham remarks, 'Mayne's self-
abasement is matched by an equal degree of resentment', but she is
perhaps unjustified in characterizing Geraldine as an 'instrument of
class cruelty',[8] since both protagonists appear to be unwitting victims
of the class system. The revealing form to which Egbert's rebellion
dwindles is a desire to enter Geraldine's social circle, a project which
enables the heroine to fantasize reassuringly about the future:

> 'When papa says to you, "My Lord the Chancellor", you will answer him
> with "A tall man, with a deep-toned voice—I know him well." When he
> says, "Such and such were Lord Hatton's words, I think", you will
> answer, "No, they were Lord Tyrrell's; I was present on the occasion";
> and so on in that way.' (*ILH*, p. 77).

As aspirant, male writer, Mayne becomes the type of what Ingham
designates 'the artist as outsider', one who is 'pressurised in a con-
sumerist society by manifestations of consumer demands'.[9] During the
five years which are supposed to have elapsed between the two parts
of the story, Egbert Mayne has attempted to enter the literary market-
place:

> It had been drive, drive from month to month; no rest, nothing but effort.
> He had progressed from newspaper work to criticism, from criticism to
> independent composition of a mild order, from the latter to the publication
> of a book which nobody ever heard of, and from this to the production of
> a work of really sterling merit, which appeared anonymously (*ILH*,
> p. 81).

Mayne becomes subtly corrupted by the very autodidactic programme
which his scheme entails, his love of the arts quenched 'by his slowly
increasing habit of looking upon each and all of these as machinery
wherewith to effect a purpose' (*ILH*, p. 82). Hardy here touches upon
the problematic insertion of a writer of humble origins into the dominant mode of literary production. In his onward progress from newspaper journalism, through periodical criticism to book production, the
protagonist, and his author, are caught up in, and subject to, a

complex set of economic, social and ideological forces. It is well known that *An Indiscretion* is based upon, or cannibalized from, Hardy's purportedly radical first work of fiction, 'The Poor Man and the Lady', written in 1867. Indeed, this novella, along with parts of *Desperate Remedies*, *Under the Greenwood Tree* and *The Hand of Ethelberta*, is all that remains of that first abortive project. *An Indiscretion* was sold to one British and two American magazines, being first published in England in the *New Quarterly Magazine* for July 1878. Egbert Mayne's career as a literary man thus refracts elements of Hardy's own experience: after 'The Poor Man and the Lady' was rejected, for instance, Hardy heeded Meredith's advice in producing the saleable sensation plot of *Desperate Remedies*. The novelist himself gives a revealingly ambivalent account of his own position around the time of the composition of *The Hand of Ethelberta*, which deals with the public and social success of a story-teller of humble origins:

> One reflection about himself at this date sometimes made Hardy uneasy. He perceived that he was 'up against' the position of having to carry on his life not as an emotion, but as a scientific game; that he was committed by circumstances to novel-writing as a regular trade, as much as he had formerly been to architecture; and that hence he would, he deemed, have to look for material in manners—in ordinary social and fashionable life as other novelists did.[10]

The development of the periodical press from the 1840s onwards marked a clear stage in the transformation of the literary product; it was a development which Hardy himself both complied with and rebelled against. The controversial status of periodical literature in relation to authors' copyright, the well-known moral intransigence of periodical editors and increasing literacy transformed the new method of publishing fiction into a cultural site of deep-seated conflict. As Norman Feltes puts it:

> What was being fought over was again not only control of the product, of the book, but also control of the labour process and of the surplus value produced in the new, fully capitalist mode of production of the modern magazine or newspaper.[11]

An adequate reading of *An Indiscretion* must demonstrate how Geraldine's virtual entrapment by the steam threshing-machine in the countryside is structurally balanced by Egbert's entrapment in the urban market-place of literature. Indeed, Feltes cites the advent of a

series of 'extraordinary machines' which transformed the publishing
process at the time—Applegarth's rotary-action press, the Hoe horizontal press, the reel-fed rotary press, and so on—and emphasizes the
new social relations which resulted from these modifications.[12] As
with the introduction of the steam threshing-machine on the land, new
methods of printing and distribution are to be construed not simply as
'moments in a steady progress towards high-speed, "modern" production but manifestations of the same process in the struggle of capitalist
enterprise towards the maximal appropriation of surplus value'.[13]
With the vogue for the magazine serialization of fiction, Feltes argues,
the writer's work begins to be reproduced within relations of production 'analogous to those prevailing in a textile mill'.[14] Such relations
affected author and reader alike, and largely contributed to those
contentious issues of textual censorship which became such a promi-
nent feature of Hardy's revisions. Indeed, the history of these transactions illustrates the curious state of independence and dependence
suffered and enjoyed by Hardy within the market.

Egbert Mayne's ambition, then, runs parallel to that of his creator.
In his novel, *Thomas Malvern* (1842), the working-class author,
Thomas Miller, makes an observation which fits both cases:

> There is a kind of neutral ground which talented authors will ever occupy;
> and although they may never become what the world calls 'gentlemen', in
> the worldly sense of the word, still they will always be received and
> treated with respect, by those who move in the highest circles of fashion-
> able society.[15]

Miller began life as a journeyman basket-weaver and was later taken
up by metropolitan literary salons. When, writing in the *Examiner* in
1876, Charles Kegan Paul referred to Hardy as one 'sprung of a race
of labouring men', the novelist corrected him with a slightly touchy
punctiliousness:

> my father is one of the last of the old 'master-masons' left. . . . From time
> immemorial—I can speak from certain knowledge of four generations—
> my direct ancestors have all been master-masons, with a set of journey-
> men masons under them: though they have never risen above this level,
> they have *never* sunk below it—i.e. they have never been journeymen
> themselves.[16]

Such self-identification with a specific village class fraction seems to
have been essential to Hardy's version of himself. It is significant that
the narrator of *An Indiscretion* insists that Egbert's father had been 'a

painter of good family, but unfortunate and improvident' (*ILH*, p. 32), in order to preserve the magazine readership from contact with a hero of working-class origins and endow Mayne's ambitions with greater plausibility. It is clear that Egbert and Hardy both share Thomas Miller's project of moving in the 'highest circles of fashionable society', and much of Hardy's covert autobiography betrays an uneasy fascination with aristocratic London society. In coming to regard art, literature and science as means of rising in society, Egbert Mayne is fully enmeshed in the operations of the literary market: the world of art and literature is identified with a specific class structure, and Egbert's incursion into the metropolis and final self-exile is symptomatic of Hardy's own problematic insertion into the cultural domain. The tensions might become overwhelming, as they were to do in *Jude the Obscure*. Egbert's attitude to art exposes the bourgeois myth of creativity which his productions must cultivate; the market rapidly compels him to consider the arts as nothing more nor less than '*machinery* wherewith to effect a purpose' (*ILH*, p. 82; italics added). In journal and book publishing at this period, commerce, advertising and literature existed cheek by jowl, and both magazines and three-deckers were predominantly aimed at a readership of middle-class women. Geraldine's literary role is thus confined to that of a reader who feels compelled to offer her congratulations when Mayne's veil of anonymity is lifted (*ILH*, p. 96). Gender categories are reinforced precisely at the point where the author appears to be questioning the fixity of class boundaries. Rachel Bowlby has argued that, in literature as elsewhere,

> women were the principal consumers of a product put out in most cases by men, and this has interesting results in terms of the types of argument used to defend or attack certain kinds of writing or the validity of readers' tastes.[17]

The profession of writer might be 'unwomanly' but could also, Bowlby suggests, be construed as 'unmanly', suggesting 'the incapacity to hold down a normal job'.[18] Whilst this incapacity certainly attaches to Egbert Mayne, Geraldine overlooks it in lauding his new-found fame (*ILH*, p. 97). Yet such momentary recognition cannot disguise the new artisanal nature of writing, and Hardy's response to this problematic position is predictably more ambiguous than that of Trollope. Mayne's engagement with the literary world, though symptomatically brief, neatly encapsulates the felt contradiction between

the figure of the artist as genius and as workman. Bowlby traces the
binding together of commerce and culture, remarking upon the paradox which transformed 'commerce into a matter of beautiful images
and culture into a matter of trade'.[19] It is partly this paradox which
leads to Egbert's retreat in an action which mimes his creator's return
from the metropolis to Dorset, or Clym's return to Egdon. In each of
these different cases, what is becoming evident is the absolute isolation
of the literary producer. The bourgeois forms and institutions open to
the hero—work or marriage—are finally experienced as constricting,
and yet it is the heroine who is sacrificed in *An Indiscretion* and *The
Return of the Native*. Hardy's novella gains much of its representative
significance from the open recognition of the relation of the writer or
artist to the mode of production, and the siting of the artist within a
determinate set of social relations. Egbert Mayne's career, that is to
say, should be read in conjunction with Hardy's complaints about the
literary market in 'Candour in English Fiction' and elsewhere.

The very anonymity of Mayne's product exemplifies the way that,
as Lukács argued in *History and Class Consciousness*, the subjects of
labour become 'rationally fragmented': 'the personality can do no
more than look on helplessly while its own existence is reduced to an
isolated particle and fed into an alien system'.[20] Just as the introduction of the steam threshing-machine will begin to transform relations
on the land, so the increasing mechanization of literary production
'destroys those bonds' which, Lukács believes, 'had bound individuals
to a community in the days when production was still "organic"'.[21]
Of course, as Lukács recognized, such an impression of atomization is
only apparent, 'the reflex in consciousness of the fact that the "natural
laws" of capitalist production have been extended to cover every
manifestation of life in society'.[22] The extension of the Allenville
estate, the arrival of the steam thresher, and the struggles of Mayne in
Grub Street are part and parcel of a single historical conjuncture
which constitutes the silence of the text, that of which it is unable to
speak.

The history of Egbert Mayne is in some sense exemplary of bourgeois aspiration in this period of accumulation, expansion and individual mobility. His rise, retreat and failure are usefully contextualized
by Chris Baldick's discussion of Marx's appropriation of the
Frankenstein myth:

> Within Marx's historical dialectic, the feverish, Cyclopean industrial
> development inaugurated in bourgeois society had necessarily to contain

the seeds of its own decline and supersession. Trapped within the property-relation, the bourgeoisie's apparently free self-assertion and confident expansion is re-read as the very hastening of its own doom.[23]

The literary treadmill, just as surely as the factory system to which it is akin, strips away the subject's illusion of freedom and creativity with the kind of awesome determinism delineated by Gissing. At the end, Egbert stands an empty cipher; the outcome of his love and ambition is a final state of emptiness which parallels the alienation effect which Marx traced in factory work, a process by which the worker, in his striking phrase, 'exists as an animated individual punctuation mark'.[24] Geraldine, as representative of an obsolescent class, is awarded the dignity of the death-bed; her lover, as aspirant bourgeois, is left to hover awkwardly in the void of his own hopes. As Baldick perceives it, the bourgeoisie, 'no longer a rational and autonomous agent in history', stands revealed 'as a haunted, *possessed* class'.[25] Egbert Mayne's return to his native countryside, therefore, is to be construed as a feeble rearguard action against the very commodification of literature in which the text of *An Indiscretion* itself unwittingly participates. Renata Poggioli's contention, that the writer 'has not yet succeeded in reconciling himself wholly to the fact that capitalist, bourgeois society tends to treat him on the one hand as a parasite and consumer and on the other hand as a worker or producer, rather than as a creator',[26] fits Mayne (and Hardy) precisely.

The narrator of *An Indiscretion*, it might be said, recites his tale in an empirical mode of naive realism which, in insisting upon a kind of truth, seems to empty the text of significance. This story of a writer specifically denies or masks its own status as writing through the controlling mastery of the narrative voice, mastery which produces a dominant but fragile discourse. *An Indiscretion* is produced out of these contradictions: it is as if Egbert Mayne were experiencing in his own career the way in which, in Lukács's phrase, 'the ceaselessly revolutionary techniques of modern production turn a rigid and immobile face towards the individual producer'.[27] The prescriptive nature of the literary market, the entrenched hegemony of the circulating libraries with their bourgeois ethical stance, and the formation of a new mass readership in the late nineteenth century afforded a set of conditions for the writer which are aptly characterized in Lukács's analysis of capitalist procedure:

man's activity does not go beyond the correct calculation of the possible
outcome of the sequence of events (the 'laws' of which he finds 'ready-
made'), and beyond the adroit evasion of disruptive 'accidents' by means
of protective devices and preventive measures.[28]

This accurately sums up both Egbert Mayne's brush with the literary
world and his creator's prolonged defensive struggle with editors and
publishers. The corrupting nature of such a process is self-evident:
speaking of Egbert's entry into literature, the narrator tells his
readers that 'several habits which he had at one time condemned in the
ambitious classes now became his own' (*ILH*, p. 82). One such revealing habit might be that larding of the text with cultural references
which is a notable feature of some Hardy texts.

Egbert Mayne's access into writing marks the cessation of speech
and the temporary ending of his relationship with Geraldine
Allenville, until he breaks his silence at the performance of *Messiah*,
only to learn of her proposed marriage to Lord Bretton. The
'perpetual strain' of the situation causes Egbert to determine 'to leave
off, for the present, at least, his efforts for distinction' in order to
'retire for a few months to his old country nook' (*ILH*, p. 100).
Retreat leads rapidly to the *dénouement*, the couple's clandestine
marriage being followed, with the illogicality of a dream, by
Geraldine's return to her irate father, and subsequent sudden death.
The effect of the hair-raising absence of causal motivation serves to
point up the arbitrariness of class discrimination, to debunk readerly
demands for a convincing handling of narrative structure and, paradoxically, to create division and dissonance through stereotypical closure. To the end, Mayne continues to occupy a subject class position,
whether waiting in the shrubbery of the great house for news of his
wife or sitting on one side of the death-bed until 'this strange family
alliance was at an end for ever' (*ILH*, p. 125). The tone is novelet-
tish, the narrative trajectory productive of bourgeois pathos. *An
Indiscretion* relies upon, and tentatively seeks to undermine, class difference. The uncertainties of Egbert Mayne appear to echo those of
Hardy himself, and the text may be read on one level as covert
revenge upon the snobbery handed out to Hardy by his father-in-law.
Certainly, it is clear that Egbert is a bourgeois intellectual whose
underlying ideology remains feudal in some sense. It is, however, in
relation to the historical moment that the compelling interest of the
tale may be located, and the tracing of such a relationship necessitates
a return to the incident which triggers off the fatal affair.

The scene of the operation of the steam threshing-machine, and the deliverance of Geraldine from the fate of becoming a 'mangled carcase' (*ILH*, p. 32), resonates beyond the exigencies of the plot. For the reader the scene must inevitably point forward to the climactic chapters of *Tess of the d'Urbervilles*, where the heroine is thrown 'into a stupefied reverie in which her arms worked on independently of her consciousness' by her job as 'feeder' to the steam thresher at Flintcomb-Ash (ch. 48). In *An Indiscretion*, significantly, the labourers are situated 'at the other part of the machine, under the cornstack some distance off' (*ILH*, p. 31). In *Tess of the d'Urbervilles* the workfolk will speak nostalgically of the days when 'everything, even to winnowing, was effected by hand-labour' (ch. 47). In both instances, the key incident dramatizes and simplifies the complex correlation of economic growth, mechanization and class domination in rural Wessex. While it is clear that the increased sophistication of hand-tools retarded mechanization on the land to a degree,[29] both of Hardy's scenes do metaphorical justice to the potency of steam power in the agricultural imagination. Indeed, Geraldine's last-minute escape rather neatly predicts the extinction of her aristocratic class role in society. As Marx observed,

> Social relations are closely bound up with productive forces. In acquiring new productive forces men change their mode of production; and in changing their mode of production, in changing the way of earning their living, they change all their social relations. The hand-mill gives you society with the feudal lord; the steam-mill, society with the industrial capitalist.[30]

That the relations between landowner, tenant farmer and labourer are every bit as harsh under feudal as under capitalist regimes is demonstrated by the accident which kills Farmer Broadford. The farmer and Egbert Mayne are, virtually, as dispossessed as the Durbeyfields themselves, and this historical process of expropriation is articulated in the operation of the new machines in both town and country. Although earlier threshing-machines had been the focal point of the 'Swing' riots of 1830, the decade of the 1850s when the story is set saw the widespread introduction of the steam threshing-machine and the mechanical harvester, with radical effect upon patterns of rural employment. In Marx's terms:

> with the introduction of machinery the division of labour inside society has increased, the task of the worker inside the workshop has been

simplified, capital has been concentrated, the human being has been further dismembered.[31]

The economics of steam power meant that a group of local farmers was compelled to hire the machinery from a firm of contractors. The introduction of new arrangements of capital investment and hire originating in the urban centres marked a turning point for farmers and labourers alike. The image of the threshing-machine in the writing project takes on an uncanny life of its own, as Marx had predicted when he urged, 'All our invention and progress seem to result in endowing material forces with intellectual life, and in stultifying human life into a material force'.[32] In such a process, he prophesied, men, women and children would be dragged, like Geraldine, 'under the Juggernaut wheels of capital':[33]

> Flush with the pond the lurid furnace burn'd
> At eve while smoke and vapour fill'd the yard;
> The gloomy winter sky was dimly starr'd,
> The fly-wheel with a mellow murmur turn'd;
> While, ever rising on its mystic stair
> In the dim light, from secret chamber borne,
> The straw of harvest, sever'd from the corn,
> Climb'd, and fell over, in the murky air.[34]

The fully fleshed-out implications of the machine are presented in *Tess of the d'Urbervilles.* Hardy's description registers a disturbed fascination with the steam thresher which anticipates the later responses to the machine espoused by modernism, notably the expressionist vision of an oppressive and destructive technology and the contrasting machine-cult of Italian Futurism or the German *Neue Sachlichkeit*:

> A panting ache ran through the rick. The man who fed was weary, and Tess could see that the red nape of his neck was encrusted with dirt and husks. She still stood at her post, her flushed and perspiring face coated with the corn-dust, and her white bonnet embrowned by it. She was the only woman whose place was upon the machine, so as to be shaken bodily by its spinning. . . . The incessant quivering in which every fibre of her frame participated had thrown her into a stupefied reverie, in which her arms worked on independently of her consciousness. She hardly knew where she was, and did not hear Izz Huett tell her from below that her hair was tumbling down (ch. 48).

In the course of an analysis of Lang's *Metropolis*, Andreas Huyssen discerns a link between female sexuality and technology which may be latently present in Hardy's writing here. In this argument, the fears and anxieties emanating from ever more powerful machines 'are recast and reconstructed in terms of the male fear of female sexuality, reflecting, in the Freudian account, the male's castration anxiety'. Although woman has commonly been read as standing closer to nature than man—an affinity which is crucial to the realization of Tess— Huyssen hypothesizes that, since the eighteenth century, nature itself 'had come to be interpreted as a gigantic machine':

> Woman, nature, machine had become a mesh of significations which all had one thing in common: otherness; by their very existence they raised fears and threatened male authority and control.[35]

Certainly both of Hardy's threshing-machine scenes derive some of their suggestiveness from what Huyssen characterizes as 'the double male fear of technology and of woman',[36] a fear which is made explicit by Alec d'Urberville's intervention at Flintcomb-Ash, and Tess's retaliatory blow with the glove. It is male domination and mastery which is at issue here as it is, more pallidly, in *An Indiscretion*. Huyssen's account is pertinent:

> Just as man invents and constructs technological artifacts which are to serve him and fulfil his desires, so woman, as she has been socially invented and constructed by man, is expected to reflect man's needs and to serve her master.[37]

Tess, dialectically constructed first as innocent victim and then as fallen woman, and Geraldine, whose only role is to inspire and energize her literary admirer, both serve the kind of reflexive role demanded of them, not only by their lovers, but also by the text. By their enforced acts of separation, both Egbert Mayne and Angel Clare work actively against the grain of their sexual desire in a movement which is designed to subdue their respective partners. The fear of technology and male alarm at the nature of female sexuality are exorcised in each narrative: in *An Indiscretion* by Egbert's gallant but enslaving rescue, in *Tess of the d'Urbervilles* by Angel's chaste return to Tess and the childlike honeymoon which precedes her execution. What is implied in *An Indiscretion* would be fully articulated in the Flintcomb-Ash sequence of *Tess of the d'Urbervilles*: the persistent domination and repression of woman works always in parallel with the domination of labour by capital and technology.

Representation of the steam threshing-machine in Hardy's fiction throws up a range of ambiguities whose origins lie within personal and social history.[38] The seemingly monstrous operations of a mechanism which would obliterate feudal class distinctions in its blind obedience to the penetrative power of capital casts a shadow over the action of both *An Indiscretion* and *Tess of the d'Urbervilles*. Hardy resolves the intractable problems thrown up by class conflict and appeases the readership in each case by recourse to a pathos of tragic individualism: the President of the Immortals, after all, appears to operate beyond the constraints of class society.

Notes

1. Millgate, *Thomas Hardy*, pp. 142-43.
2. P. Widdowson, *Hardy in History* (London: Routledge, 1989), pp. 131-32.
3. P. Ingham, *Thomas Hardy* (London: Harvester Wheatsheaf, 1989), p. 48.
4. Widdowson, *Hardy in History*, p. 147.
5. Widdowson, *Hardy in History*, p. 148.
6. Widdowson, *Hardy in History*, p. 149.
7. Widdowson, *Hardy in History*, p. 216.
8. Ingham, *Thomas Hardy*, pp. 50, 52.
9. Ingham, *Thomas Hardy*, p. 55.
10. *Life*, p. 107.
11. N.N. Feltes, *Modes of Production of Victorian Novels* (Chicago: University of Chicago Press, 1986), p. 59.
12. Feltes, *Modes of Production*, p. 60.
13. Feltes, *Modes of Production*, p. 61.
14. Feltes, *Modes of Production*, p. 63.
15. Cited in N. Cross, *The Common Writer* (Cambridge: Cambridge University Press, 1985), p. 127.
16. *Collected Letters*, I, p. 89.
17. R. Bowlby, *Just Looking* (London: Methuen, 1985), p. 89.
18. Bowlby, *Just Looking*, p. 89.
19. Bowlby, *Just Looking*, p. 9.
20. G. Lukács, *History and Class Consciousness* (trans. R. Livingstone; London: Merlin Press, 1971), p. 90.
21. Lukács, *History*, p. 90.
22. Lukács, *History*, pp. 91-92.
23. C. Baldick, *In Frankenstein's Shadow* (Oxford: Oxford University Press, 1987), p. 127.
24. Karl Marx, *Grundrisse* (trans. M. Nicolaus; Harmondsworth: Penguin Books, 1973), p. 470.
25. Baldick, *Frankenstein's Shadow*, p. 127.
26. R. Poggioli, 'The Artist in the Modern World', in *The Sociology of Art and*

Literature (ed. M. Albrecht *et al.*; London: Gerald Duckworth, 1970), p. 674.

27. Lukács, *History*, p. 97.

28. Lukács, *History*, p. 98.

29. On the improvement in hand-tools, see E.J.T. Collins, 'Harvest Technology and Labour Supply in Britain, 1790–1870', *The Economic History Review* 22 (1969), pp. 453-73.

30. Karl Marx, 'The Poverty of Philosophy', in Karl Marx and Friedrich Engels, *Collected Works*, VI (London: Lawrence & Wishart, 1976), p. 166.

31. Marx, 'Poverty of Philosophy', p. 188.

32. Speech on the jubilee celebration of *The People's Paper*, in Karl Marx and Friedrich Engels, *Collected Works*, XIV (London: Lawrence & Wishart, 1980), p. 656.

33. Karl Marx, 'Value, Price and Profit', in *The Essential Left* (London: Unwin, 1960), p. 94.

34. Charles Tennyson Turner, 'The Steam Threshing-Machine' (1868).

35. A. Huyssen, *After the Great Divide* (London: Macmillan, 1986), p. 70.

36. Huyssen, *Great Divide*, p. 71.

37. Huyssen, *Great Divide*, pp. 71-72.

38. Dorchester became a centre for steam-driven agricultural machines in the early 1870s when Francis Eddison set up his works at Fordington. Hardy objected to the sounding of the factory hooter at 5.45 a.m. every working day.

Chapter 6

'THE DORSETSHIRE LABOURER' (1883)

Hardy's essay on the Dorset labourer is a quintessentially readerly text. The overall tendency of his article is to reduce the field-labourer to a passive effect of the prose. Whilst Hardy is at pains to redeem the fieldworker from the public stereotype available in the 'pitiable picture known as Hodge' (*PW*, p. 168), the writing itself enforces a version of cultural unity which depends upon a kind of hegemonic discourse for its persuasiveness. Raphael Samuel has pertinently remarked on the fact that the nineteenth-century village labourer 'remains a curiously anonymous figure',[1] and the underlying project of Hardy's overtly sympathetic text is to sustain and reinforce that anonymity. The voice of the labourer is dispersed through subtle textual effects, with the result that the journalistic essay takes on the form of one of those texts which indicates by its very conventions the way it is to be consumed.

In arguing against the tendency towards stereotyping, at the outset of the essay Hardy imagines a gentlemanly 'investigator' who seeks out a remote rural community and spends six months in a worker's cottage. The rational voice here mediates between reader and rustic, passes judgment on localized conflicts and converts dialect speech into an urbanely neutral prose:

> The great change in his perception is that Hodge, the dull, unvarying, joyless one, has ceased to exist for him. He has become disintegrated into a number of dissimilar fellow-creatures, men of many minds, infinite in difference; some happy, many serene, a few depressed; some clever, even to genius, some stupid, some wanton, some austere; some mutely Miltonic, some Cromwellian; into men who have private views of each other, as he has of his friends; who applaud or condemn each other; amuse or sadden themselves by the contemplation of each other's foibles or vices; and each of whom walks in his own way the road to dusty death (*PW*, pp. 170-71).

The stance, echoed in the balanced and contrastive clauses, is that of judicious observer. The kind of compromises involved in such a stance have been well registered by Raymond Williams:

> the political relations of the observer–observed, where the 'language-habits' studied, over a range from the speech of conquered and dominated peoples to the 'dialects' of outlying or socially inferior groups, theoretically matched against the observer's 'standard', were regarded as at most 'behaviour', rather than independent, creative, self-directing life.[2]

Does Hardy's project here, that is to say, possess a much greater insight or validity than Clym Yeobright's? The standpoint in the essay is closely akin to what Eagleton, in a discussion of Hardy's fiction, describes as 'a form of dual seeing, equally ambivalent in its relation of subject and object'. The labourers depicted in the novels, as Eagleton remarks, exist within an acute contradiction between 'a sense of themselves as uniquely individual' and a sense of themselves mediated 'by an observer's vantage point'.[3] Immediately prior to the passage cited, Hardy insists upon the vitality of the demotic. The imaginary observer, he argues, would quickly discover that peasant speech, far from being 'a vile corruption of cultivated speech', was a language which had been compelled to mix the 'printed tongue' with the 'unwritten, dying, Wessex English' (*PW*, p. 170). The elegiac tone is symptomatic of Hardy's dilemma: he deplores the imposition of a uniform, standardized English, while participating in such an imposition. That linguistic uniformity is a necessary precondition for the formation of capitalist enterprise has been persuasively argued by Pierre Macherey and the Balibars.[4] Such uniformity was achieved through the mechanical instilling of the rules of classical grammar into the children of the workfolk, a process which produced an apparent equality between speakers which served to obscure marginality and dispossession. As Macherey and the Balibars have shown, literary texts such as Hardy's essay work unconsciously to enforce bourgeois domination through language. In the essay, indeed, class conflict and ideological contradiction is masked by such suave formulations as this:

> A pure atmosphere and a pastoral environment are a very appreciable portion of the sustenance which tends to produce the sound mind and body, and thus much sustenance is, at least, the labourer's birthright (*PW*, p. 171).

At these points in the text the reader may perceive a mythical Wessex in the process of production, a cultural commodity being prepared for ideological consumption. Hardy's notion of the workfolk is indeed a curiously passive one. He reads their historical situation as that of victims; being now taught at the new National Schools, for instance, the children of the poor produce 'a composite language without rule or harmony' (*PW*, p. 170). Hardy's essay possesses little sense of the radical or creative potential of dialectal or linguistic change. Against this lack, it is pertinent to balance Raymond Williams's insistence upon language not as 'a *tradition* to be learned', nor 'a set of meanings which, because it is "our language", has a natural authority', but as 'a shaping and reshaping, in real circumstances and from profoundly different and important points of view'. Whereas Williams stresses the ways in which men and women 'go on making [their] own language and history',[5] Hardy is concerned largely to express a sense of inevitable process and change in which the field-labourers are ineluctably caught up. It is through language that this difference of emphasis and interpretation is inscribed. Williams sees language as an active participant in a history of material practices—the kind of practices in which the Dorset fieldworkers were engaged throughout a long period of expropriation and protest. In such a view, language-formation is a site of conflict where different material interests state their separate claims to hegemony and meaning. Hardy, on the other hand, views linguistic and social change through the lens of evolutionary law, developing sequentially with inevitable displacement and loss. In a letter to the *Spectator* written two years before the essay, Hardy deployed the vocabulary of Darwinism to describe what was happening. Standard English, he argued, had become the 'all-prevailing competitor'; by contrast, regional dialects were 'worsted in the struggle for existence, when a uniform tongue became a necessity among the advanced classes of the population' (*PW*, p. 93). The permeation effect of standard English compelled a retreat of dialect forms into secluded rural areas and led to widespread dialect bilingualism. The influence of cultivated speech upon folk speech is a complex matter, but it is clear that, for the speech patterns of the rural working class, the influence of the Board Schools which were set up after 1870 was to be crucial. Schoolteachers introduced a new model for the written language, while the old speech habits might prevail at home. Mrs Durbeyfield habitually speaks the local dialect, but her daughter, who has passed the sixth standard in the National School, 'spoke two languages; the dialect at home, more or less; ordinary English abroad and to persons of quality' (*Tess of the d'Urbervilles*, ch. 3). Such linguistic sedimentation evidently also affected a more educated kind of speaker: in *Jude the Obscure*, the narrator notes of Phillotson and Gillingham that these 'well-trained and even proficient masters' would occasionally use 'a dialect-word of their boyhood to each other in private' (Pt IV, ch. 3). The speech community formed by the workfolk of Dorset became increasingly compelled to bridge the gap between itself and that wider speech community which espoused standard English. The rustics of Egdon exist within a dialect relic zone in which the old forms still predominate, whilst Tess and Phillotson inhabit a linguistic transition zone in which differing linguistic forms coexist.

The kind of shifts and stresses involved here are sharply registered in Captain Vye's animadversions upon the deleterious effects of the new village schools, on the occasion of Clym Yeobright's return to Egdon:

> 'Strange notions, has he?' said the old man. 'Ah, there's too much of that sending to school in these days! It only does harm. Every gatepost and barn's door you come to is sure to have some bad word or other chalked upon it by the young rascals: a woman can hardly pass for shame sometimes. If they'd never been taught how to write they wouldn't have been able to scribble such villainy. Their fathers couldn't do it, and the country was all the better for it.' (*The Return of the Native*, Bk II, ch. 1).

Elsewhere, Hardy would remove from his text a heavily non-standard English speech given by Henchard when elevated to mayor (*The Mayor of Casterbridge*, ch. 5), and paradoxically allow Henchard to display his anger when Elizabeth-Jane lapses into dialect. Such instances, which had begun with Fancy Day's admonition of her father's speech on her wedding day, illustrate the contradictory social and class situations thrown up by the cultivation of standard forms of speaking and writing.[6] The contradictions observable in rural Dorset might be said to be produced by a kind of slow-motion version of the effects noted by Samuel Bamford in newly industrialized Lancashire. Bamford speaks of the consequences of 'the breaking up of old associations and the formation of new ones', as a result of which 'new modes of dress became common; new modes of living were adopted; new subjects of thinking were started'. Such a process led to linguistic modification and the introduction of new words; it is from that juncture, Bamford observes, that 'the old dialect, with the old customs of the country and the old fashions, has been gradually receding towards oblivion'.[7]

The overall effect of Hardy's analysis is to elide the class antagonism, the gap between 'dark' and 'official' village, which permeated rural society at this juncture of severe agricultural depression. Here is Joseph Arch:

> At the sight of the squire the people trembled. He lorded it right feudally over his tenants, the farmers; the farmers in their turn tyrannised over the labourers; the labourers were no better than toads under a harrow. Most of the farmers were oppressors of the poor; they put on the iron wage-screw, and screwed the labourer's wages down, down below living point; they stretched him on the rack of life-long abject poverty.[8]

By contrast, Hardy's procedure is to deconstruct the lineaments of such poverty, want and dispossession through an analysis which is significantly optical in effect. A cottage in which 'the walls, the furniture, and the dress of the inmates reflect the brighter rays of the solar spectrum' is 'read' by philanthropic visitors as 'a cleanly, happy home', in contradistinction to one 'whose prevailing hue happens to be dingy russet', which is thought 'necessarily the abode of filth' (*PW*, p. 172). This 'inability to see below the surface of things' (*PW*, p. 173) enables Hardy to reassure the gentlemanly readers of *Longman's Magazine* in 1883 that true poverty is 'constantly trying to be decent' (*PW*, p. 174). In contrast, Hardy goes on to imagine the Dorset labourer at 'his worst and saddest time', attending a hiring-fair on a wet Candlemas (*PW*, p. 174). Again, Hardy's account is visually submissive in its comparison between contemporary and earlier fairs:

> A glance up the high street of the town on a Candlemas-fair day twenty or thirty years ago revealed a crowd whose general colour was whity-brown flecked with white. Black was almost absent, the few farmers who wore that shade hardly discernible. Now the crowd is as dark as a London crowd. This change is owing to the rage for cloth clothes which possesses the labourers of today (*PW*, p. 175).

Both men and women rendered thus become 'pictorially, less interesting than they used to be' (*PW*, p. 176). The effect of such a passage, and of the ensuing description of the Lady Day migrations, a version of which Hardy later inserted into *Tess of the d'Urbervilles*, is to provide a curiously de-historicized and reified version of social change devoid of those 'structures of feeling' which might evoke some sense of lived experience from the point of view of the labourers themselves. Such reification in Hardy's texts produces what Eagleton characterizes as a 'form of schizophrenia' in which 'the socially visible aspect of men and women—their bodies—seems wholly sundered from their living identities'.[9] The 'social content' of the act of looking, as Fredric Jameson has argued in relation to colonialism, is an affirmation of the observer's dominating superiority, a process through which 'the objects of the surrounding world can be effectively mastered and visually enumerated'.[10] The 'special kind of inspection inherent in the obsessive visual survey', of which Hardy's essay is an instance, is possessed of a particular 'social significance': what Jameson designates the 'genealogy of the gaze' finds its origins in 'that first commercial world of the primitive accumulation of capital'.[11] Thus it is that the 'apparently purely formal disembodied compulsion of the gaze' secretes within it a deep-seated 'political and economic content'.[12] The writing of the essay simultaneously speaks for, and silences, a social group which lacks its own public articulation, and in its descriptive fullness notably fails to provide the kind of analysis which would expose and examine the structuration of consciousness through material conditions. The essay, Hardy's most overtly sociological text, represents an aestheticized response to its subject. It is one of those works which, in Eagleton's terms, is tied to 'an ideology which silences it at certain points'.[13] History, the history of land tenure, wage labour, enclosure and dispossession, becomes the other of the text, its absent subject, articulated in the interstices of its realist-descriptive mode. Such a mode privileges perception at the expense of the imperceptible social relations which produce those acts of perception.

Hardy, characteristically, reads the hiring-fair semiotically. Like the men, the women are also 'less interesting' than heretofore:

> Instead of the wing bonnet like the tilt of a waggon, cotton gown, bright-hued neckerchief, and strong flat boots and shoes, they (the younger ones at least) wear shabby millinery bonnets and hats with beads and feathers, 'material' dresses, and boot-heels almost as foolishly shaped as those of ladies of highest education (*PW*, p. 176).

As Raymond Williams remarks, signs come to take on the 'changed and often reversed social relations of a given society', to the extent that they become emblems of 'the contradictory and conflict-ridden social history of the people who speak the language'.[14] Hardy, pertinently remarking that 'Change is also a certain sort of education', believes that with the increase in movement the workfolk are 'losing their peculiarities as a class' (*PW*, p. 180). Progress and 'picturesqueness' do not 'harmonise' evidently, and the end-result is 'a less intimate and kindly relation with the land' (*PW*, p. 181): rootlessness leads to anonymity. Despite, or because of, the sympathetic tone and dispassionate voice, it is hard not to feel that the labouring man or woman has disappeared from the text. As E.P. Thompson has noted, the problems of focus and identity in such analyses are formidable:

> In all this very difficult tangle of conflicting evidence—between the effect of the Poor Laws here and new potato patches there, this lost common right and that cottage garden—the 'average' labourer proves more than elusive.[15]

Certainly the uprooting of the tenantry and copyholders which Hardy depicts here, and inscribes in the plots of *The Woodlanders* and *Tess of the d'Urbervilles*, was widely commented upon in the period. Engels, for instance, observed that farm-hands had become day-labourers, 'employed only when needed by the farmers';[16] and, writing from within an antithetical tradition, George Bourne described the cottager deprived of common rights as 'a broken man—a peasant shut out from his countryside and cut off from his resources'.[17]

It is indicative of the contradictions in Hardy's position that, in alluding to Joseph Arch, he feels the need to refer to Arch's origins in a mythicized Shakespearean landscape where, readers are assured, 'the humours of the peasantry have a marked family relationship with those of Dorset men' (*PW*, p. 183). By drawing upon a received comic tradition, Hardy softens and blurs the radicalism of the agrarian 'Revolt of the Field', and its potential for a shift in the ownership of land and production of food. Hardy is at pains to emphasize the 'remarkable moderation' of Arch's language (*PW*, p. 184), so as to produce a homogeneous image of rural life for his middle-class audience. Rural depopulation and the consequent alterations in village life-patterns occupy Hardy in the final pages of the essay, but in his conclusion he is content to sidestep the issues raised, arguing somewhat limply that 'the question of the Dorset cottager here merges in that of all the houseless and landless poor' (*PW*, p. 189). The contradictions implicit in the essay arise out of the role of language as a material force within the reproduction of capitalism: Hardy's prose unwittingly becomes complicit with a desire to structure the world in accordance with a market economy. In his *Annals of the Labouring Poor*, K.D.M. Snell argues cogently for the case that boundaries need to be carefully set as to what a writer 'may know and be able to express of his society and its social structure', so as to understand 'in what areas his knowledge is likely to be limited, occluded, or distorted'.[18] Hardy's stress upon the newly migratory form of fieldwork is queried in Snell's account, which argues that this annual hiring system had long provided 'an institutional nexus for mobility via the statute fairs'. Snell goes on,

> The historical alienation from a 'primal', local sense of place which Hardy depicted as occurring in his own lifetime, supposedly affecting 'the old-fashioned stationary sort' of rural labourer, was. . . based on a nostalgic fiction of the past: on the notion of an original unity and its subsequent break-up.[19]

The Dorset labourer is effectively silenced in the seamless flow of Hardy's meditative prose. When the labourers found a voice, as in Alexander Somerville's interviews published in *The Whistler at the Plough* (1852), their conversation was marked by bitterness and class animosity. Such direct reportage speaks eloquently of the 'subjective feelings and experience of farm labourers in a way never found in Hardy', revealing a range of discontents such as 'the game-laws, low wages, pretentious living standards of the farmers, or the bad diet'.[20] Against the calmly evolutionary perspective of change evoked and manipulated by Hardy, Snell's account focuses upon crisis and fracture:

> From Tolpuddle on throughout the nineteenth century, in literary and blue book reportage, the Dorset agricultural labourer was associated with about the most squalid and depressed living standards to be found in England, and the most embittered class relations.[21]

Snell's assertion that, in his fiction, Hardy 'was concerned with the agricultural labourer in only a very marginal fashion',[22] is open to question, as is his discovery of a 'comic and derisory Hodge, with an occasional touch of ludicrous magniloquence'.[23] Yet it is hard, with all allowances made, not to concur with the judgment that, in reading Hardy's work, 'landowning and tenant farmer classes could readily ignore their guilt over the condition of the labourer'.[24] Snell's conclusion that the novels 'rarely enter seriously and sympathetically into the area of labourers' values, priorities, and subjective experience', and that they are 'revealingly reticent on the actual conditions of life in Dorset',[25] challenges a long tradition of reading Hardy. But it is unequivocally clear to the reader of 'The Dorsetshire Labourer' that, as Snell puts it, Hardy's 'aspirant class mobility is apparent in his descriptive prose'.[26] The history of Hardy's own 'sort of education' may be the key to the unruffled contradictions of the essay. As John Goode points out, Hardy's relationship to the work of writing is dialectical: 'it is both an institution which has to be negotiated and an agency of self-improvement'.[27] That upward social mobility was, necessarily, bought at a cost, as Hardy recognized in his portraits of Clym Yeobright or Jude Fawley. The relation which Goode proposes between writing as institution and agency complicates Hardy's project in unforeseeable ways. In addressing the plight of the Dorset field-labourer he had also to address a journal-reading public, part of that middle class which Engels judged to be the most 'deeply demoralised', 'incurably debased by selfishness' and 'corroded within' of any in Europe.[28]

Hardy, it is clear, is anxious to produce a balanced effect in his essay; yet the very concept of balance is shot through with ideological contradictions and political implications. The adoption of a middle ground, in this case between the labouring classes and the landowners and tenant-farmers, bears a close resemblance, as John Barrell points out, 'to a certain ideal construction of the situation of the middle-class—neither aristocratic nor progressive'. The notion of balance itself becomes, in such analyses, 'a term of value with a crucial function in middle-class ideology, underwriting the political authority of "consensus", or the "middle ground"'.[29]

It is only by reading against the grain of the essay that some of the contradictions of Hardy's prose may be resolved or articulated. Bakhtin's exploration of the way the grounding of values takes place in the I/other distinction, a distinction which reproduces the economic formation, helps to account for the essentially monologic nature of Hardy's discourse in the essay. The life experience of the field-men and women of Dorset, in Bakhtin's phrase, 'lives a tense life on the borders of someone else's thought, someone else's consciousness'.[30] The strategic placing of the workfolk, the distancing implicit in Hardy's judicious tone of voice in what he designates 'a merely descriptive article' (PW, p. 189), reduces them to objects of contemplation. Such a ploy may be interrogated by means of Bakhtin's contention that the subject 'cannot be perceived or studied as if it were a thing, since it cannot remain a subject if it is voiceless'. There is, therefore, 'no knowledge of the subject but *dialogical*'.[31] The reader of Hardy's essay needs to listen for what Bakhtin terms 'a counter-discourse to the discourse of the utterer'.[32] But such is the power of the master discourse that the historic struggles of the farm-labourers are manifestly 'already penetrated by the other's intentions'. The labourer's own intention 'finds a word already lived in'.[33] The conflict of material conditions, the daily stress of living experienced by nineteenth-century field-men and women, is also simultaneously a struggle for language, for the articulation of value and meaning. Against the hegemonic monoglossia of Hardy's piece, a productive reading of the essay will, in Bakhtin's telling phrase, 'hear *voices* everywhere'[34]—those voices which have been largely silenced by a written culture divorced from direct material production. Hardy, like other commentators upon the plight of the rural poor in the period, remains partially deaf to such voices; it is in these lacunae, in what Eagleton terms the 'gaps and absences' of the text, that ideology is fully revealed. Eagleton's remarks, indeed, are of particular relevance to the experience of reading the Dorset labourer essay:

> The text is, as it were, ideologically forbidden to say certain things; in trying to tell the truth in his own way, for example, the author finds himself forced to reveal the limits of the ideology within which he writes. He is forced to reveal its gaps and silences, what it is unable to articulate. Because a text contains these gaps and silences, it is always *incomplete*.[35]

Bakhtin's conception of language as an intersection of voices, of writing as a dialogue between several writings, opens up and exposes the elision and incompleteness of Hardy's analysis. Meaning is not fixed; rather, the text is a site of that struggle which permeates all material practice, from harvesting, hedging and ditching, or swede-cutting, to writing and publishing. Hardy's inscription here memorial-izes, celebrates and immobilizes the primarily oral culture of the village labourer, which could find no voice in the pages of a metro-politan gentleman's magazine. In Raymond Williams's words, such a culture 'cannot be expressed or substantially verified in terms of the dominant culture',[36] a culture with which Hardy found himself in an increasingly uneasy relationship. Indeed, that culture is itself, as Bakhtin puts it, 'furrowed with distant and barely audible echoes of changes of speech subjects and dialogic overtones, greatly weakened utterance boundaries which are completely permeable to the author's expression'.[37] In both the essay and those areas of his fiction which deal with the working people, Hardy is involved in a project of trans-lation, locating his writing midway between differing cultural and linguistic patterns. Such permeation effects are observed more clearly in Hardy's fictional rendering of the speech and experience of the workfolk than in the essay itself. The essay, taking its meaning from its historical moment of production, projects a monologic, centralizing containment of otherness and a censorship of historical suffering, dispossession and mobilization. In the novels, the author is compelled by the nature of his material to enter into a more clearly articulated dialogue with the working people. The conversations of the furze-cutters in *The Return of the Native*, dominated by the speech-memories of Timothy Fairway or Grandfer Cantle, insert a distinctive folk voice and record into the hectic actions of the higher-class characters. Here, for example, is Fairway's account of the death of the elder Yeobright:

> 'However, then she went on, and that's what made me bring up the story, "Well, whatever clothes I've won, white or figured, for eyes to see or for eyes not to see" ('a could do a pretty stroke of modesty in those days), "I'd sooner have lost it than have seen what I have. Poor Mr Yeobright was took bad directly he reached the fair ground, and was forced to go home again." That was the last time he ever went out of the parish.'
> ' 'A faltered on from one day to another, and then we heard he was gone.'
> 'D'ye think he had great pain when 'a died?' said Christian.
> 'Oh no: quite different. Nor any pain of mind. He was lucky enough to be God A'Mighty's own man.'
> 'And other folk—d'ye think 'twill be much pain to 'em, Mister Fairway?'
> 'That depends on whether they be afeard.'
> 'I bain't afeard at all, I thank God!' said Christian strenuously. 'I'm glad I bain't, for then t'won't pain me. . . I don't think I be afeard—or if I be I can't help it, and I don't deserve to suffer. I wish I was not afeard at all!'
> (Bk I, ch. 5).

In Hardy's rendering of patterns of folk speech, as Eagleton observes, 'a subjective human life emerges from beneath the distancing, impenetrable exterior'.[38] While such a scene in some senses dialogizes the situation of author, reader and the workfolk who act as subjects, the effective dialogism is scrupulously limited. Hardy was careful to adopt a literary version of dialect, believing that 'if a writer attempts to exhibit on paper the precise accents of a rustic speaker he disturbs the proper balance of a true representation by unduly insisting upon the grotesque element', as he told the *Athenaeum* in 1878. The 'chief concern' of such writing is the idealist one of depicting 'men and their natures rather than their dialect forms' (*PW*, p. 91). Bakhtin's remarks, in *The Dialogic Imagination*, upon Onegin's language are relevant in this case. Fairway's language may be characterized as 'a period-bound language associated with a particular world-view', or 'an image that speaks'. Like Pushkin, Hardy is 'far from neutral' in his relationship to this image; on the contrary, he 'argues with it, agrees with it. . . interrogates it, eavesdrops on it, but also ridicules it, parodically exaggerates it, and so forth'. In other words, the author is in a dialogical relation with Fairway's language; such a convention is, Bakhtin argues, 'the fundamental constitutive element of all novel-istic style'.[39] It is this dialogic principle which is productive of the type of heteroglossia which inhabits a text like *The Return of the Native*, but which is scrupulously excluded from the Dorset labourer essay. In the conflictual relationship between regional dialect and standard English, the novel unconsciously mirrors and re-works issues of class-division and a history of appropriation and centralization. Bakhtin remarks, 'one's own language is never a single language: in it there are always survivals of the past and a potential for other-languagedness that is more or less sharply perceived by the working literary and language consciousness'.[40]

The tension which Bakhtin identifies in the struggle between cen-tripetal and centrifugal forces in the formation of a national language places novels like *The Return of the Native* or *Tess of the d'Urbervilles* 'on the border between the completed, dominant literary language and the extraliterary languages that know heteroglossia'.[41] While Hardy's essay necessarily speaks from and for the dominant, 'completed' language, the novel, by definition, situates itself upon a borderland which admits, however mutedly, other voices, other his-tories. In the exchanges between Fairway, Humphrey, Sam, Christian and Grandfer Cantle and the others, Hardy skilfully draws upon folk-loric forms and tropes. Within such forms, a central role has histori-cally been assigned to the rogue, the fool and the clown. Such figures possess, Bakhtin argues, a metaphorical significance for the work in which they appear. Indeed, their outward appearance, 'everything they do and say', cannot be understood 'in a direct and unmediated way', but is to be 'grasped metaphorically'. As Hardy demonstrates in the mumming episode, such personages are what Bakhtin designates 'life's maskers': 'their being coincides with their role, and outside this role they simply do not exist'.[42] Such masks are 'rooted deep in the folk', and serve to overturn the 'vulgar conventionality' attributable to the kind of 'feudal ideology' which pervades Egdon. The 'level-headed, cheery and clever wit' (Fairway), 'the parodied taunts of the clown' (Grandfer Cantle), and the 'simpleminded incomprehension of the fool' (Christian) stand in opposition to middle-class convention.[43] Such characters function as a force for exposure of idealism and sublimation, whether in the bogus projects of Clym Yeobright, the romantic sublimities of Eustacia, or the maternal possessiveness of Mrs Yeobright. The workfolk of Egdon, by contrast, emerge from 'the deep recesses of pre-class folklore', serving to re-establish what Bakhtin calls 'literature's sundered tie with the public square', and exposing to public gaze the vulgarity of bourgeois personal life, 'down to its most private and prurient little secrets'.[44] In the speech of the fool, Bakhtin argues, 'lies a polemical failure to understand someone else's discourse, someone else's pathos-charged lie'—that lie which, like Clym's, 'has appropriated the world and aspires to conceptualize it'.[45] In such episodes as the debate about Christian's inability to attract women, the dance to greet the returning Yeobright, or the wild village 'gipsying' into which Eustacia and Wildeve are drawn, Hardy mobilizes precisely those forms of which Bakhtin speaks, 'for making public all unofficial and forbidden spheres of human life', in particular 'the sphere of the sexual and of vital body functions (copulation, food, wine)'.[46] Indeed, in the memorable folk activities recorded in the novel, such as the bonfire-lighting, the mumming play, or the dance episodes, Hardy studiously memorializes what Bakhtin characterizes as 'the time of holidays and ceremonies connected with the agricultural labour cycle, with the seasons of the year, the periods of the day, the stages in the growth of plants and cattle'. In such cycles, time is 'differentiated and measured only by the events of *collective* life', a life which 'works itself out in a collective battle of labour against nature'.[47] Set against this life of mutuality, labour and public exposure, Hardy depicts his middle-class protagonists. Bakhtin has traced the ways in which, from the middle ages onwards, the 'gross realities of the ancient pre-class complex' split and differentiated themselves, elements being reallocated between 'high' and 'low'. In such a process, sexuality, in its 'realistic and straightforward aspect', is 'driven out of the official genres and out of official discourse', to reappear in the sublimated form of bourgeois love.[48] Out of that 'common time of collective life' inhabited by the furzecutters, Bakhtin traces the emergence of 'separate individual lifesequences, individual fates',[49] such as those delineated in the careers of Yeobright, his mother, Wildeve, Thomasin and Eustacia.

By drawing upon the potent categories of clown and fool, the voices of carnival, Hardy seeks to avert the reader's gaze from the facts of labour on the heath, from the daily grind of furze-cutting in all weathers, poverty, squalid living conditions and dispossession. While the actions of the collectivity of the workfolk provide the novel with some of its finest scenes, these actions are significantly always related to holiday or feast. The economic basis of fuel-provision and sale for the Egdonites is elided here: the only furze-cutter whom the reader sees hard at work turns out to be Clym Yeobright, as seen through the eyes of Eustacia. The effect of such a description is to transform economic imperative into bourgeois pathos; in contradistinction to, for instance, Levin's joyful participation in the communal work of scything in *Anna Karenina*, the stress here is upon isolation and indignity:

> He was busily chopping away at the furze, a long row of faggots which stretched downward from his position representing the labour of the day. He did not observe her approach, and she stood close to him, and heard his under-current of song. It shocked her. To see him there, a poor afflicted man, earning money by the sweat of his brow, had at first moved her to tears; but to hear him sing and not at all rebel against an occupation which, however satisfactory to himself, was degrading to her, as an educated lady-wife, wounded her through (Bk IV, ch. 2).

The passage exercises a quite subtle appeal to both class and gender prejudice in the implied reader. Linked to the telling description of Clym's 'microscopic' closeness to the nature of the heath, such a passage caters to readerly desire while remaining silent about the facts of human labour and class conflict on Egdon.

By contrast, the talk of the workfolk is imbued with life and energy. Here, for instance, they discuss Christian Cantle's sexual shortcomings:

> 'Yes, "No moon, no man." 'Tis one of the truest sayings ever spit out. The boy never comes to anything that's born at new moon. A bad job for thee, Christian, that you should have showed your nose then of all days in the month.'
>
> 'I suppose the moon was terrible full when you were born?' said Christian, with a look of helpless admiration at Fairway.
>
> 'Well, 'a was not new', Mr Fairway replied, with a disinterested gaze.
>
> 'I'd sooner go without drink at Lammas-tide than be a man of no moon', continued Christian, in the same shattered recitative. ' 'Tis said I be only the rames of a man, and no good for my race at all; and I suppose that's the cause o't.'
>
> 'Ay', said Grandfer Cantle, somewhat subdued in spirit; 'and yet his

mother cried for scores of hours when 'a was a boy, for fear he should outgrow hisself and go for a soldier.' (Bk I, ch. 3).

In such dialogue, Bakhtin contends, the 'concrete utterance of a speaking subject serves as a point where centrifugal as well as centripetal forces are brought to bear'. Processes of centralization and decentralization, of unification and disunification, here 'intersect' potently. The utterance of the Egdonites, that is to say, 'participates in the "unitary language"', but at the same time 'partakes of social and historical heteroglossia'.[50] The essay, by contrast, is a more purely rhetorical form, monologic in its compositional structure, and thus 'oriented toward the listener and his answer'.[51] In the novel, Bakhtin argues, 'dialogisation penetrates from within the very way in which the word conceives its object'.[52] Although the word is always 'half someone else's',[53] in the essay the word has been wholly wrested away from the folk, appropriated to Hardy's own semantic and expressive intentions. Yet language remains fundamentally heteroglot. As Bakhtin explains, the 'illiterate peasant' who lives 'miles away from any urban centre', 'naively immersed', like the Egdonites, in an 'unmoving' world, inhabits several languages simultaneously—prayer, song, family gossip, official communication and so on. The workfolk, Bakhtin remarks, can pass 'from one to the other without thinking, automatically'.[54] Such acts of linguistic transgression are everywhere recorded in the dialogue of Hardy's rustic characters. The novels, taken as authorial utterance, assume the form of what Bakhtin characterized as 'never-ending, internally unresolved dialogues among characters (seen as embodied points of view) and between the author himself and his characters'. Placed within such a dialogic form, the discourse of the labourers is 'never entirely subsumed and remains free and open'.[55]

By comparison, when Hardy treats of the workfolk in the essay, the reader is brought face to face with what Bakhtin designates 'a literary and language consciousness operating from the heights of its own uncontestably authoritative unitary language',[56] in a discourse which fails to countenance heteroglossia. In such writing the field-labourers exist as objects of discourse, just as economically they exist as the property of others. Yet while the essay typifies the way in which, in Bakhtin's account, everything which cannot be conceptualized 'is ordered on the template of convention, smoothed out, straightened, polished, touched up',[57] in the version of its final paragraphs which was inserted into *Tess of the d'Urbervilles* it works to quite opposite effect:

> dragging what is being compared down to the dregs of an everyday gross reality congealed in prose, thereby destroying the lofty literary plane that had been achieved by polemical abstraction. Here heteroglossia avenges itself for having been excluded and made abstract.[58]

The Durbeyfields' expulsion from Marlott is given substance and historical context by Hardy's careful re-working of part of the closing section of his essay. A discourse which, in the bland confines of a gentleman's magazine, works to create one meaning, to serve one class interest, slightly shifts its emphasis in a different system of intertextual relations. 'The Dorsetshire Labourer' may, that is to say, be reproduced to effect a changed set of meanings. Whereas the essay, at the moment of its first publication, serves a current orthodoxy of humanism by claiming a factual truth-content, and by its failure to unmask the prevailing view of the agricultural question, in the embodiment of fiction it works to reveal the way misrecognition of social relations is embedded in bourgeois ideology. The passage recontextualized in chapter 51 of *Tess of the d'Urbervilles* exposes to middle-class gaze that genuine knowledge of its own objective class-position in relation to production which is scrupulously avoided in the essay on the same subject. When Hardy, in the midst of the action of *Tess of the d'Urbervilles*, speaks of 'the mutations so increasingly discernible in village life' (ch. 51), and embodies those mutations in the life experience of Tess and her family, he brings about in the readership a renewed attentiveness to the conditions of village life. There is a more compelling social truth negotiated in the fiction than in the 'factual' essay. 'The Dorsetshire Labourer' functions differently according to its context, in ways which have been explicated by Tony Bennett:

> There is no pure text, no fixed and final form of the text which conceals a hidden truth which has but to be penetrated for criticism to retire, its task completed. There is no once-and-for-all, final truth about the text which criticism is forever in the process of acquiring. The text always and only exists in a variety of historically concrete forms.[59]

In its homogeneously anodyne discursive mode in *Longman's Magazine*, the essay conforms to Bennett's analysis of the way literary practice 'constitutes an essentially ideological operation in its attempts to heal or placate class and ideological contradictions inscribed within language itself':[60]

The pleasures enjoyed by the Dorset labourer may be far from pleasures of the highest kind desirable for him. They may be pleasures of the wrong shade. And the inevitable glooms of a straitened hard-working life occasionally enwrap him from such pleasures as he has; and in times of special storm and stress the "Complaint of Piers the Ploughman" is still echoed in his heart. But even Piers had his flights of merriment and humour; and ploughmen as a rule do not give sufficient thought to the morrow to be miserable when not in physical pain (*PW*, p. 171).

In this kind of passage Hardy both patronizes and distances his subject; the effect of a kind of rote-learned journalistic phraseology—'storm and stress', 'sufficient thought to the morrow'—in combination with a tone of unassailable generalization is to blot out the lineaments of historic suffering. What was the identity of labourers? Where were their voices to be heard? The nineteenth-century farm-labourers remain, in Hardy's characteristic analysis, unheard. As E.J. Hobsbawm and George Rudé observed in *Captain Swing*, it is a deafening symptomatic silence:

Who were they? Nobody except themselves and the rulers of their villages knew or cared, nobody except the clergyman or (much more rarely) dissenting minister entered the few basic facts of their obscure lives in the parish register: birth, marriage and death.[61]

Although Hardy, in the essay and at times in the novels, accepts the necessity of change, and even cites the union agitation of the 1870s as one instrument of that process, the final implication of the essay is undoubtedly a looking back to a rural society characterized by Hobsbawm and Rudé as 'traditional, hierarchical, paternalist, and in many respects resistant to the full logic of the market'.[62] In the transformation of field labour registered in the contrasting scenes of harvesting at Marlott and the steam-threshing at Flintcomb-Ash, Tess experiences in her own career the widespread proletarianization of the farmworker with which Hardy seems to grapple unsuccessfully in the essay. Looking back to the formative years which led up to the machine-breaking and incendiarism of 1830, Hobsbawm and Rudé comment,

Instead of the village community (as symbolised by open field and common) there was now enclosure. Instead of mutual aid and social obligation, there was now the Poor Law, administered exclusively by the rulers of the countryside. Instead of family, patronage or custom, there was now the straightforward nexus of wages, which bound the landless to the landed.[63]

This perspective, for all its backward glance to a more stable situation, does not, as the authors note, imply that 'the communal institutions and customs of the countryside were egalitarian' in that earlier period.[64] The contrast between Marlott and Flintcomb-Ash is not a simplistically imagined representation of the difference between a communal and an individualist ethic. Marlott, though without a great landowner, is a village in which the relation of labourer to landlord is as harsh and unremitting as that experienced by Tess and her fellow workers under Mr Groby at Flintcomb-Ash. It is the very anonymity of the Marlott landlord which renders the expulsion of the Durbeyfields after the death of 'Sir John' all the more stark in its dramatization of the economic imperative. In a quasi-feudal hierarchy the facts of material expropriation may, temporarily, be masked; at Flintcomb-Ash these facts stand nakedly revealed. The contrast is not between hand- and machine-labour but between implicit and explicit forms of economic exploitation.

Agrarian change in the nineteenth century in southern Britain meant that workers gradually became a group set apart from their employers. The rise of bigger work-teams which were irregularly employed, and the tendency of the larger farmer to become an entrepreneur, made the employer more remote. This growing segregation had been compounded by the development in the late eighteenth century of 'open' and 'close' parishes. In a 'close' parish the number of labouring families was controlled by the owners of property and the parish vestry so as to limit the number of persons eligible for poor-relief. Many day-labourers were thus forced to live at a distance from their work in an 'open' parish. The countryside began to see a separation of the labourers from the employer into a community antipathetic to him. This gradual separation enabled the growth of a genuine working-class culture which Hardy's essay evades. Through a network of meeting places—public house, friendly societies, benefit clubs, poaching gangs and so on—the field-labourer found a voice. It was in this context, one largely ignored in Hardy's novels except in its comic potential, that agricultural protest and action grew up. It was in Tess's own Vale of Blackmoor, as Barbara Kerr has demonstrated,[65] that some of the most determined attacks on the threshing-machines took place in 1830; Kerr characterizes the overall situation of the work-force in Dorset thus:

With the apathy of undernourished men the labourers tolerated a system
which just enabled them to exist but bound them to a servile dependence
on their employers and the parish overseers.[66]

Prior to unionism it was very difficult for labourers to get a wage
claim acknowledged. Hardy, indeed, comments upon the rise of wages
brought about by the 'agitation', and reflects upon the irony that, if
the farmer could now be prevailed on to pay 30 per cent higher wages
and still live well in a time of depression, then 'the labourer must have
been greatly wronged' in earlier days (*PW*, p. 184).[67] Economic
insight, however, soon gives place in the essay's drift to a more
generalized set of reflections upon the differences between male and
female employment in the countryside. It is a pervasive characteristic
of the essay that it presents the field-labourer as a victim of circumstances. Hardy fails to delineate or imagine for his readership the
emergence of any specifically working-class movement with its own
life and culture. The essay skilfully evades, or glosses over, the one
demand Benjamin deems essential for the writer: 'the demand to
think, to reflect upon his position in the production process'.[68]
Compelling reasons for such silence may be sought through an examination of the writer's class position. Hardy was born into that inter-
mediate class fraction composed of lifeholders and copyholders who
were sometimes small farmers, often craftsmen and artisans, and
occasionally a mixture of both. Widdowson comments upon the
'complex and shifting position of the class of Hardy's origins', arguing
that Hardy both belonged to and felt alienated from 'a class fraction
which is itself in a precarious position in the larger structure of the
rural social economy'.[69] This precariousness bears further examination in relation to the situating of the reader by the rhetorical effects
of Hardy's essay on the Dorset labouring class. Historiographical
orthodoxy has tended to elide the functional significance of the class of
small farmers and tradespeople to which the Hardys belonged in
favour of a polarized social formation envisaged as a site of contestation between landed and farming capital and workpeople. Agrarian
change, it is clear, did create a landless proletariat; but there remained
many dual-occupation families which utilized their capital and their
labour to create wealth. Such families might be linked to the small
farmer by ties of kinship, financial dependence, or religious or political affiliation. Although the rural labourer in mid-nineteenth-century
England was subject to power relations at home and at work,
nevertheless, as Mick Reed has suggested, the intricacy of village class

relations meant that the exercise of power was mediated:

> laws, rules, and instructions were interpreted by persons or groups whose
> interests were not uniform and were often opposed. What has often been
> called the 'collective conspiracy of the village rich', is a tempting but over-
> simplified notion, since the rich themselves were not always united, and
> were opposed not only by the labourers but often by those who actually
> administered the rulings of the rich.[70]

Within both open and closed parishes, small farmers, tradespeople and
even labourers, Reed argues, 'were able to sustain agricultural under-
takings, greater and more diverse than would seem possible at first
sight'.[71] Hardy's father belonged precisely to that class fraction which
was not directly implicated, but lived athwart, the capitalist reorgani-
zation of land and labour which proceeded spasmodically throughout
the period. While such a group might count themselves with the
bourgeoisie economically—Hardy's father, after all, was a small-scale
employer of labour—they were often opposed to the gentry and the
larger farmers in other matters. The collusion of the artisanal village
class in middle-class notions of 'progress', and the unfettered development of capital during the period embraced contradiction and
provisionality.

Such ambivalence was heightened, in Hardy's case, by the upward
social mobility afforded by education and writing. Literature, as
Widdowson observes, offered Hardy a field in which the powerful
sense of social inferiority which entry into the middle class usually
entailed did not apply. The voice of the Dorset labourer essay is, to
some extent, that of the lower-class rural man who, as Widdowson
remarks, 'has entered the educated and privileged domain of a
metropolitan cultural class, and cannot admit his origins'.[72] Hardy's
perspective was deeply marked by the high social mobility characteristic of the late Victorian period, which may be associated with the
Board Schools. His entry into the metropolitan literary scene was, in
the case of 'The Poor Man and the Lady', both radical and defensive.
The tone of patronage which intermittently enters his work is
produced, not out of snobbery, but rather out of Hardy's own experience of class mobility with its attendant anxiety. It is, precisely, the
discrepant nature of Hardy's social perspective which produces the
fertile ambiguity of the fiction and the flawed weakness of the sociological essay. As Macherey argues, the writer is 'involved in the
movement of his age', but is necessarily unable to produce a complete
account:

The writer is not there to articulate the total structure of an epoch; he gives us, rather, an image, a unique and privileged glimpse. This privilege derives from his social position, as individual and as writer. The role of the writer, you might say, is to dramatise the historical structure by narrating it.[73]

But whereas Macherey is able to define Tolstoy's relationship to the history of his time by tracing the elaboration, by a member of the gentry class, of a doctrine of peasant solidarity, such a reversal is never available to Hardy. The authorial voice, both in the essay and in the fiction, oscillates between differing class positions and sympathies; indeed, the writing is the effect of such oscillation, the record of a continuous internal dialogue. Hardy is, as it were, both more progressive and more conservative than Tolstoy in his rendition of rural change. His *déclassé*, observer's stance is often bought at the cost of a bland condescension to the workfolk in both essay and fiction; yet his membership of that fluid artisanal class fraction invests his examination of the formation of a rural proletariat, in *Tess of the d'Urbervilles* or *Jude the Obscure*, with genuine authority. A historical period does not spontaneously produce a monolithic ideology. It is rather the case, Macherey has argued, that the literary work must be encountered within a kind of double perspective, 'in relation to history, and in relation to an ideological version of that history'.[74]

The agricultural unionism of the early 1870s arose with marked rapidity, and was ostensibly motivated by urban agitation for a nine-hour day, and by an upsurge of rural employment in a rising market. But underlying the movement assiduously cultivated by Arch and his Warwickshire combinations lay the memory of Captain Swing, Tolpuddle and the Rebecca riots. The 'Revolt of the Field' of 1872, which led to an agricultural union membership of 150,000, was strongly felt in eastern Dorset; it was less effective in the west of the county where hiring fairs were few, and where the railway had not penetrated. Nationally, wages were raised by about 30 per cent, but within two years the unions were in disarray, and the farmers were successfully organizing lock-outs.[75] Hardy's essay, in the last analysis, cannot bring itself to speak of these matters in its depiction of the plight of the propertyless. The overall effect upon the reader is of a grave wringing of hands over the spectacle of change. Yet the field-men and women were at that time engaged in a struggle to improve their lot and affirm their rights. The problematic question of how an apparently alienated and brutalized rural proletariat could gain an insight into the organization of production and, by creating their own class consciousness, become capable of political action, is not faced here; it would surface ambiguously in the Flintcomb-Ash sequence of *Tess of the d'Urbervilles.* 'The Dorsetshire Labourer' does not ultimately afford the farm-labourer his or her own voice. The evidence of the collective protests of agricultural workers is here elided or rendered a subject of bourgeois pathos. As Raymond Williams pertinently remarked, 'for all the talk of degeneration of the labourer', what is perhaps most remarkable about this 'terrible period' is 'a development of spirit and of skill'. Speaking of those very agricultural labourers who were ostensibly the subject, but in reality became the object, of Hardy's essay, Williams goes on,

> What impresses me most, because it is a creative spirit, is their courage and their willingness to act, their finding of actions which would have some effect, in a cause of relieving extreme poverty and hunger which anyone now (but now does not count; their children were hungry then) would support.[76]

In contemplating the problems inherent in forging a connection between the economy of the relations of production and the economy of the subject, Barthes posed the question, 'what is the relation between class determination and the unconscious?' The proletariat, he argued, 'may well be mute'—as it is in Hardy's essay—'but it still speaks in the discourse of the intellectual, not as canonical founding voice but as unconscious'.[77] As the Other, the unconscious, the rural proletariat would haunt Hardy's discourse to the end of his career as a writer.

Notes

1. R. Samuel, 'Village Labour', in *Village Life and Labour* (ed. R. Samuel; London: Routledge & Kegan Paul, 1975), p. 3.

2. R. Williams, *Marxism and Literature* (Oxford: Oxford University Press, 1977), p. 27.

3. T. Eagleton, 'Thomas Hardy: Nature as Language', *Critical Quarterly* 13 (1971), p. 160.

4. See E. Balibar and P. Macherey, 'On Literature as an Ideological Form', in *Untying the Text* (ed. R. Young; London: Routledge & Kegan Paul, 1981); R. Balibar, 'An Example of Literary Work in France', in *The Sociology of Literature: 1848* (ed. F. Barker *et al.*; Colchester: University of Essex Press, 1978);

R. Balibar, 'National Language, Education, Literature', in *Literature, Politics and Theory* (ed. F. Barker *et al.*; London: Methuen, 1986).

5. R. Williams, *Keywords* (London: Fontana, 1976), p. 22.
6. See R. Williams, *The Long Revolution* (London: Chatto & Windus, 1961); T. Crowley, *The Politics of Discourse* (London: Macmillan, 1989); R. Chapman, *The Language of Thomas Hardy* (London: Macmillan, 1990).
7. S. Bamford, *Dialect of South Lancashire* (1850), cited in B. Sharratt, *Reading Relations* (Brighton: Harvester, 1982), p. 241.
8. J. Arch, *The Life of Joseph Arch by Himself* (1898), cited in *Class and Conflict in Nineteenth Century England* (ed. P. Hollis; London: Routledge & Kegan Paul, 1973), p. 123.
9. Eagleton, 'Nature as Language', p. 160.
10. F. Jameson, 'Modernism and its Repressed', in *The Ideologies of Theory*, I (Minneapolis: University of Minnesota Press, 1988), p. 173.
11. Jameson, 'Modernism', p. 173.
12. Jameson, 'Modernism', pp. 173-74.
13. T. Eagleton, *Marxism and Literary Criticism* (London: Methuen, 1976), p. 35.
14. R. Williams, *Politics and Letters* (London: New Left Books, 1979), p. 176.
15. E.P. Thompson, *The Making of the English Working Class* (Harmondsworth: Penguin Books, 1968), p. 237.
16. Friedrich Engels, *The Condition of the Working Class in England* (London: Panther, 1969), p. 287.
17. G. Bourne, *Change in the Village* (Harmondsworth: Penguin Books, 1984), p. 79.
18. K.D.M. Snell, *Annals of the Labouring Poor* (Cambridge: Cambridge University Press, 1987), p. 374.
19. Snell, *Annals*, p. 379.
20. Snell, *Annals*, pp. 383, 386.
21. Snell, *Annals*, pp. 386-87.
22. Snell, *Annals*, p. 388.
23. Snell, *Annals*, p. 388.
24. Snell, *Annals*, p. 390.
25. Snell, *Annals*, p. 392.
26. Snell, *Annals*, p. 397.
27. J. Goode, *Thomas Hardy: The Offensive Truth* (Oxford: Basil Blackwell, 1988), p. 142.
28. Engels, *Condition*, p. 301.
29. J. Barrell, *Poetry, Language, Politics* (Manchester: Manchester University Press, 1988), pp. 5-6.
30. Bakhtin, *Dostoevsky's Poetics*, p. 32.
31. Bakhtin, cited in T. Todorov, *Mikhail Bakhtin: The Dialogical Principle* (trans. W. Godzich; Manchester: Manchester University Press, 1984), p. 18.
32. Todorov, *Bakhtin*, p. 22.
33. Todorov, *Bakhtin*, p. 48.
34. Todorov, *Bakhtin*, p. 21.

35. Eagleton, *Marxism and Literary Criticism*, p. 35.

36. Williams, *Marxism and Literature*, p. 122.

37. Bakhtin, cited in *Bakhtin: Essays and Dialogues on his Work* (ed. G.S. Morson; Chicago: University of Chicago Press, 1986), p. 97.

38. Eagleton, 'Nature as Language', p. 156.

39. M.M. Bakhtin, *The Dialogic Imagination* (ed. M. Holquist: trans. C. Emerson and M. Holquist; Austin: University of Texas Press, 1981), p. 46.

40. Bakhtin, *Dialogic Imagination*, p. 66.

41. Bakhtin, *Dialogic Imagination*, p. 67.

42. Bakhtin, *Dialogic Imagination*, p. 159.

43. Bakhtin, *Dialogic Imagination*, p. 162.

44. Bakhtin, *Dialogic Imagination*, pp. 165, 163.

45. Bakhtin, *Dialogic Imagination*, p. 403.

46. Bakhtin, *Dialogic Imagination*, pp. 165-66.

47. Bakhtin, *Dialogic Imagination*, pp. 206-207.

48. Bakhtin, *Dialogic Imagination*, p. 213.

49. Bakhtin, *Dialogic Imagination*, p. 214.

50. Bakhtin, *Dialogic Imagination*, p. 272.

51. Bakhtin, *Dialogic Imagination*, p. 280.

52. Bakhtin, *Dialogic Imagination*, p. 284.

53. Bakhtin, *Dialogic Imagination*, p. 293.

54. Bakhtin, *Dialogic Imagination*, pp. 295-96.

55. Bakhtin, *Dialogic Imagination*, p. 349.

56. Bakhtin, *Dialogic Imagination*, p. 368.

57. Bakhtin, *Dialogic Imagination*, p. 380.

58. Bakhtin, *Dialogic Imagination*, p. 386.

59. T. Bennett, *Formalism and Marxism* (London: Methuen, 1979), p. 148.

60. Bennett, *Formalism*, p. 161.

61. E.J. Hobsbawm and G. Rudé, *Captain Swing* (Harmondsworth: Penguin Books, 1973), p. xvii.

62. Hobsbawm and Rudé, *Captain Swing*, p. xxi.

63. Hobsbawm and Rudé, *Captain Swing*, p. 17.

64. Hobsbawm and Rudé, *Captain Swing*, p. 17.

65. B. Kerr, *Bound to the Soil* (London: John Baker, 1968), ch. 5.

66. Kerr, *Bound to the Soil*, p. 99.

67. In his history of the farm-labourer Alan Armstrong observes that, at the time, the 'Revolt of the Field' was widely regarded as 'a long overdue reaction to oppression and conditions of wretchedness'. In discussing the relative rise in labourers' wages, Armstrong pertinently notes that when the Earl of Yarborough died in 1875 his stock of cigars was sold for £850, 'more than 18 years' income for a Lincolnshire agricultural worker' (Alan Armstrong, *Farmworkers* [London: Batsford, 1988], pp. 109, 133).

68. Walter Benjamin, *Understanding Brecht* (London: Verso, 1983), p. 101.

69. Widdowson, *Hardy in History*, pp. 131-32.

70. M. Reed, 'The Peasantry of Nineteenth-Century England: A Neglected Class?', *History Workshop* 18 (1984), p. 64.
71. Reed, 'Peasantry', p. 58.
72. Widdowson, *Hardy in History*, p. 138.
73. Macherey, *Literary Production*, p. 113.
74. Macherey, *Literary Production*, p. 115.
75. See J.P.D. Dunbabin, 'The Revolt of the Field', *Past and Present* 24-26 (1963), pp. 68-97.
76. Williams, *The Country and the City*, p. 184.
77. Barthes, *Image, Music Text*, p. 212.

BIBLIOGRAPHY

Armstrong, A., *Farmworkers* (London: Batsford, 1988).

Bakhtin, M.M., *Problems of Dostoevsky's Poetics* (trans. C. Emerson; Manchester: Manchester University Press, 1988).

—*The Dialogic Imagination* (ed. M. Holquist: trans. C. Emerson and M. Holquist; Austin: University of Texas Press, 1981).

Baldick, C., *In Frankenstein's Shadow* (Oxford: Oxford University Press, 1987).

Balibar, E., and P. Macherey, 'On Literature as an Ideological Form', in *Untying the Text* (ed. R. Young; London: Routledge & Kegan Paul, 1981).

Balibar, R., 'An Example of Literary Work in France', in *The Sociology of Literature: 1848* (ed. F. Barker *et al.*; Colchester: University of Essex Press, 1978).

—'National Language, Education, Literature', in *Literature, Politics and Theory* (ed. F. Barker *et al.*; London: Methuen, 1986).

Barrell, J., *Poetry, Language, Politics* (Manchester: Manchester University Press, 1988).

Barthes, R., 'Baudelaire's Theatre', in *A Barthes Reader* (ed. S. Sontag; London: Jonathan Cape, 1982).

—*Image, Music, Text* (trans. S. Heath; London: Fontana, 1977).

—*Roland Barthes by Roland Barthes* (trans. R. Howard; London: Macmillan, 1977).

—*S/Z* (trans. R. Miller; London: Cape, 1975).

—*The Pleasure of the Text* (trans. R. Miller; New York: Noonday Press, 1975).

Bayley, J., *An Essay on Hardy* (Cambridge: Cambridge University Press, 1978).

Belsey, C., *Milton* (Oxford: Basil Blackwell, 1988).

Benjamin, W., *Charles Baudelaire* (trans. H. Zohn; London: Verso, 1983).

—*Illuminations* (ed. H. Arendt; trans. H. Zohn; London: Fontana, 1973).

—*Moscow Diary* (ed. G. Smith; trans R. Sieburth; Cambridge, MA: Harvard University Press, 1986).

—*One-Way Street and Other Writings* (trans. E. Jephcott and K. Shorter; London: Verso, 1985).

—*The Origin of German Tragic Drama* (trans. J. Osborne; London: Verso, 1985).

—*Understanding Brecht* (London: Verso, 1983).

Bennett, T., *Formalism and Marxism* (London: Methuen, 1979).

Blanchot, M., *The Sirens' Song* (ed. G. Josipovici; trans. S. Rabinovitch; Brighton: Harvester, 1982).

Bloom, C., *The Occult Experience and the New Criticism* (Brighton: Harvester, 1986).

Bloom, H., *The Anxiety of Influence* (Oxford: Oxford University Press, 1975).

Bourne, G., *Change in the Village* (Harmondsworth: Penguin Books, 1984).

Bowlby, R., *Just Looking* (London: Methuen, 1985).

Brady, K., *The Short Stories of Thomas Hardy* (London: Macmillan, 1982).

Chapman, R., *The Language of Thomas Hardy* (London: Macmillan, 1990).

Collins, E.J.T., 'Harvest Technology and Labour Supply in Britain, 1790–1870', *The Economic History Review* 22 (1969), pp. 453-73.

Coward, R., and J. Ellis, *Language and Materialism* (London: Routledge & Kegan Paul, 1977).

Cross, N., *The Common Writer* (Cambridge: Cambridge University Press, 1985).

Crowley, T., *The Politics of Discourse* (London: Macmillan, 1989).

Derrida, J., *Glas* (Paris: Galilée, 1974).

—*Of Grammatology* (trans. G.C. Spivak; Baltimore: Johns Hopkins University Press, 1976).

—*Writing and Difference* (trans. A. Bass; London: Routledge & Kegan Paul, 1978).

Docherty, T., *On Modern Authority* (Brighton: Harvester, 1987).

Dunbabin, J.P.D., 'The Revolt of the Field', *Past and Present* 24-26 (1963), pp. 68-97.

Eagleton, T., 'Thomas Hardy: Nature as Language', *Critical Quarterly* 13 (1971), pp. 155-62.

—*Marxism and Literary Criticism* (London: Methuen, 1976).

—*Walter Benjamin* (London: Verso, 1981).

Eliot, T.S., *After Strange Gods* (London: Faber & Faber, 1934).

—*Selected Prose* (ed. J. Hayward; Harmondsworth: Penguin Books, 1953).

Engels, F., *The Condition of the Working Class in England* (London: Panther, 1969).

Feltes, N.N., *Modes of Production of Victorian Novels* (Chicago: University of Chicago Press, 1986).

Foucault, M., 'What is an Author?', in *The Foucault Reader* (ed. P. Rabinow; Harmondsworth: Penguin Books, 1986).

—*Discipline and Punish* (trans. A. Sheridan; Harmondsworth: Penguin Books, 1979).

—*Language, Counter-Memory, Practice* (trans. D.F. Bouchard and S. Simon; Ithaca, NY: Cornell University Press, 1977).

—*The Archaeology of Knowledge* (trans. A. Sheridan Smith; London: Tavistock Publications, 1974).

—*The History of Sexuality*, I (trans. R. Hurley; Harmondsworth: Penguin Books, 1981).

—*The Order of Things* (London: Tavistock Publications, 1974).

Freud, S., 'Family Romances', in *On Sexuality* (ed. A. Richards; trans J. Strachey; Harmondsworth: Penguin Books, 1977).

—'The Dynamics of Transference', in *The Standard Edition of the Complete Psychological Works*, XII (trans. J. Strachey; London: Hogarth Press, 1958).

—*The Interpretation of Dreams* (ed. A. Richards; trans. J. Strachey; Harmondsworth: Penguin Books, 1976).

—*Totem and Taboo* (trans. A.A. Brill; Harmondsworth: Penguin Books, 1938).

Gallop, J., *Feminism and Psychoanalysis: The Daughter's Seduction* (London: Macmillan, 1982).

Gatrell, S., *Hardy the Creator* (Oxford: Clarendon Press, 1988).

Gittings, R., *Young Thomas Hardy* (Harmondsworth: Penguin Books, 1978).

Goode, J., *Thomas Hardy: The Offensive Truth* (Oxford: Basil Blackwell, 1988).

Gribble, J., *The Lady of Shalott in the Victorian Novel* (London: Macmillan, 1983).

Hardy, T., *The Life and Work of Thomas Hardy* (ed. M. Millgate; London: Macmillan, 1984).

Hazlitt, W., *The Spirit of the Age* (ed. E.D. Mackerness; London: Collins, 1969).

Hillis Miller, J., *Thomas Hardy: Distance and Desire* (Cambridge, MA: Harvard University Press, 1970).

—'Thomas Hardy, Jacques Derrida, and the "Dislocation of Souls" ', in *Taking Chances: Derrida, Psychoanalysis and Literature* (ed. J. Smith and W. Kerrigan; Baltimore: Johns Hopkins University Press, 1984).

Hobsbawm, E.J., and G. Rudé, *Captain Swing* (Harmondsworth: Penguin Books, 1973).

Huyssen, A., *After the Great Divide* (London: Macmillan, 1986).

Ingham, P., *Thomas Hardy* (London: Harvester Wheatsheaf, 1989).

Irigaray, L., 'Sexual Difference', in *French Feminist Thought* (ed. T. Moi; Oxford: Basil Blackwell, 1987).

Jameson, F., 'Modernism and its Repressed', in *The Ideologies of Theory*, I (Minneapolis: University of Minnesota Press, 1988).

Kerr, B., *Bound to the Soil* (London: John Baker, 1968).

Kristeva, J., 'On the Melancholic Imaginary', in *Discourse in Psychoanalysis and Literature* (ed. S. Rimmon-Kenan; London: Methuen, 1987).

Lacan, J., *Ecrits* (trans. A. Sheridan; London: Tavistock Publications, 1980).

—*The Four Fundamental Concepts of Psychoanalysis* (trans. A. Sheridan; Harmondsworth: Penguin Books, 1986).

Lawrence, D.H., *Study of Thomas Hardy and Other Essays* (ed. B. Steele; Cambridge: Cambridge University Press, 1985).

Lloyd, C., *The British Seaman* (London: Paladin, 1970).

Lukacher, N., *Primal Scenes* (Ithaca, NY: Cornell University Press, 1986).

Lukács, G., *The Historical Novel* (Harmondsworth: Penguin Books, 1969).

—*History and Class Consciousness* (trans. R. Livingstone; London: Merlin Press, 1971).

Mabey, R. (ed.), *Landscape with Figures: An Anthology of Richard Jefferies's Prose* (Harmondsworth: Penguin Books, 1983).

MacCannell, J.F., *Figuring Lacan* (London: Croom Helm, 1986).

Macherey, P., *A Theory of Literary Production* (trans. G. Wall; London: Routledge & Kegan Paul, 1978).

Man, P. de, *Allegories of Reading* (New Haven: Yale University Press, 1979).

—*Blindness and Insight* (London: Methuen, 1983).

—*The Rhetoric of Romanticism* (New York: Columbia University Press, 1984).

Marx, K., 'The Poverty of Philosophy', in K. Marx and F. Engels, *Collected Works*, VI (London: Lawrence & Wishart, 1976).

—'Value, Price and Profit', in *The Essential Left* (London: Unwin, 1960).

—*Grundrisse* (trans. M. Nicolaus; Harmondsworth: Penguin Books, 1973).

Millgate, M., *Thomas Hardy* (Oxford: Oxford University Press, 1985).

Moi, T., *Sexual/Textual Politics* (London: Methuen, 1985).

—(ed.), *The Kristeva Reader* (Oxford: Basil Blackwell, 1986).

Morson, G.S. (ed.), *Bakhtin: Essays and Dialogues on his Work* (Chicago: University of Chicago Press, 1986).

Mulvey, L., *Visual and Other Pleasures* (London: Macmillan, 1989).

Poggioli, R., 'The Artist in the Modern World', in *The Sociology of Art and Literature* (ed. M. Albrecht *et al.*; London: Gerald Duckworth, 1970).

Purdy, R.L., *Thomas Hardy: A Bibliographical Study* (Oxford: Clarendon Press, 1978).

Purdy, R.L., and M. Millgate, *The Collected Letters of Thomas Hardy*, I (Oxford: Clarendon Press, 1978).

—*The Collected Letters of Thomas Hardy*, VI (London: Clarendon Press, 1987).

Reed, M., 'The Peasantry of Nineteenth-Century England: A Neglected Class?', *History Workshop* 18 (1984), pp. 53-76.

Rignall, J., 'Benjamin's *Flâneur* and the Problem of Realism', in *The Problems of Modernity: Adorno and Benjamin* (ed. A. Benjamin; London: Routledge, 1989).

Rose, J., *Sexuality in the Field of Vision* (London: Verso, 1986).

Ryan, M., *Marxism and Deconstruction* (Baltimore: Johns Hopkins University Press, 1982).

Samuel, R., 'Village Labour', in *Village Life and Labour* (ed. R. Samuel; London: Routledge & Kegan Paul, 1975).

Showalter, E., *The Female Malady* (London: Virago, 1987).

Snell, K.D.M., *Annals of the Labouring Poor* (Cambridge: Cambridge University Press, 1987).

Stallybrass, P., and A. White, *The Politics and Poetics of Transgression* (London: Methuen, 1986).

Thompson, E.P., *The Making of the English Working Class* (Harmondsworth: Penguin Books, 1968).

Todorov, T., *Mikhail Bakhtin: The Dialogical Principle* (trans. W. Godzich; Manchester: Manchester University Press, 1984).

Weeks, J., *Sex, Politics and Society* (London: Longman, 1981).

White, H., *Metahistory* (Baltimore: Johns Hopkins University Press, 1973).

Widdowson, P., *Hardy in History* (London: Routledge, 1989).

Williams, R., *The Long Revolution* (London: Chatto & Windus, 1961).

—*The Country and the City* (London: Chatto & Windus, 1973).

—*Keywords* (London: Fontana, 1976).

—*Marxism and Literature* (Oxford: Oxford University Press, 1977).

—*Politics and Letters* (London: New Left Books, 1979).

Wolff, J., 'The Invisible Flâneuse', in *The Problems of Modernity: Adorno and Benjamin* (ed. A. Benjamin; London: Routledge, 1989).

Woolf, V., *A Room of One's Own* (Harmondsworth: Penguin Books, 1963).

—*Collected Essays* (London: Hogarth Press, 1968).

Wotton, G., *Thomas Hardy: Towards a Materialist Criticism* (Dublin: Gill & Macmillan, 1985).

INDEXES

GENERAL INDEX

Adorno, T.W. 40
Ainsworth, H. 15
Albrecht, M. 127
Arch, J. 133, 135, 149, 151
Arendt, H. 41
Armstrong, A. 152

Bakhtin, M. 8, 92, 107, 137-41, 143, 152
Baldick, C. 120, 121, 126
Balibar, E. 130, 150
Balibar, R. 130, 150
Bamford, S. 132, 151
Barker, F. 151
Barrell, J. 137, 151
Barthes, R. 7, 9, 16, 39, 60, 64-66, 69-72, 90, 101, 104, 106, 108, 150, 153
Bass, A. 106
Baudelaire, C. 34, 40, 41, 108
Bayley, J. 13, 39, 92, 107
Belsey, C. 66, 71
Benjamin, A. 40
Benjamin, W. 33-37, 40, 41, 64, 65, 71, 85, 97, 104, 106-108, 147, 152
Bennett, T. 144, 152
Binswanger, L. 14
Blanchot, M. 100, 107
Bloom, C. 30, 31, 40
Bloom, H. 15, 39
Bonaparte, N. 43, 47, 49, 57, 58
Bouchard, D.F. 108
Bourne, G. 135, 151
Bowlby, R. 119, 120, 126
Braddon, M.E. 15
Brady, K. 73, 74, 106
Brecht, B. 152

Brill, A.A. 107
Browning, R. 94

Carlyle, T. 61
Chapman, R. 151
Charcot, J.-M. 97, 98
Coleman, T. 10
Collins, E.J.T. 127
Collins, W. 15
Coward, R. 72
Cromwell, O. 61
Cross, N. 126
Crowley, T. 151

De Man, P. 13-15, 39, 95, 103, 104, 107, 108
Derrida, J. 15, 17, 39, 75, 76, 88, 101, 102, 106, 108
Docherty, T. 78, 79, 106
Dunbabin, J.P.D. 153

Eagleton, T. 34, 35, 41, 130, 133, 134, 138, 139, 150-52
Ebbatson, R. 10
Eddison, F. 127
Eliot, G. 15
Eliot, T.S. 92, 98, 101, 107, 108
Ellis, J. 72
Emerson, C. 107, 152
Engels, F. 33, 127, 135, 137, 151

Feltes, N. 117, 118, 126
Fielding, H. 106
Ford, D. 61
Foucault, M. 39, 41, 49, 50, 60, 91, 92, 98, 101, 107, 108

Freud, S. 16, 21, 39, 40, 54, 57, 65, 89, 94, 97, 106, 107
Furbank, P.N. 10

Gallop, J. 40, 72, 89, 90, 106
Gatrell, S. 108
Gibson, J. 10
Gifford, E. 111
Gifford, J.A. 111
Gissing, G. 121
Gittings, R. 98, 107
Godzich, W. 151
Goode, J. 137, 151
Gribble, J. 60

Hardy, M.H. 43
Hardy, Sir T.M. 43, 49, 53, 58
Hayward, J. 108
Hazlitt, W. 47, 59
Heath, S. 71
Henniker, A. 86
Henniker, F. 86, 87, 91, 108
Hill, S. 10
Hobsbawm, E.J. 145, 152
Hollis, P. 151
Holquist, M. 152
Howard, R. 39
Hurley, R. 106
Hutchins, J. 105
Huyssen, A. 124, 125, 127

Ibsen, H. 107
Ingham, P. 112, 116, 126
Irigaray, L. 20, 22, 40, 57, 65, 71

Jameson, F. 134, 151
Jefferies, R. 33, 40
Jephcott, E. 40
Josipovici, G. 107

Kafka, F. 74, 75
Keats, J. 86
Kerr, B. 146
Kerrigan, W. 106
Kristeva, J. 67-70, 72, 91, 107

Lacan, J. 8, 22, 25, 26, 28, 40, 54, 55, 60

Lang, F. 33, 124
Lawrence, D.H. 55, 60, 113
Livingstone, R. 126
Lloyd, C. 60
Lucretius 15
Lukacher, N. 35, 37, 41
Lukács, G. 47, 59, 120, 121, 126, 127
Luxembourg, R. 8

Mabey, R. 40
MacCannell, J.F. 25, 26, 40
Macherey, P. 7-9, 15, 39, 130, 148-50, 152, 153
Mackerness, E.D. 59
Martin, J.A. 21
Marx, K. 120, 121, 123, 124, 126, 127
Meredith, G. 15, 117
Miller, J.H. 52, 59, 60, 74, 75, 106
Miller, R. 9, 60
Miller, T. 118, 119
Millgate, M. 21, 40, 59, 86, 87, 106-108, 126
Milton, J. 71, 103
Moi, T. 40, 57, 60, 67, 68, 70-72
Morson, G. 151
Mulvey, L. 23, 40
Mussolini, B. 57

Nicolaus, M. 126

Orel, H. 10
Osborne, J. 41

Paul, C.K. 118
Poe, E.A. 34
Poggioli, R. 121, 126
Proust, M. 97
Purdy, R.L. 40, 59, 71, 72
Pushkin, A. 140

Rabinovitch, S. 107
Rabinow, P. 107
Reed, M. 147, 148, 153
Régnier, H. de 108
Richards, A. 39, 40
Rignall, J. 34, 40, 41
Rimmon-Kenan, S. 107
Rose, J. 67, 70, 72, 97, 107

Rudé, G. 145, 152
Ryan, M. 9

Samuel, R. 130, 150
Scott, W. 47
Shakespeare, W. 13, 103
Sharratt, B. 151
Shelley, P.B. 15, 86, 90, 104
Sheridan, A. 40, 60, 107
Shorter, K. 40
Showalter, E. 89, 98, 106, 107
Sieburth, R. 107
Simon, S. 108
Smith, G. 107
Smith, J. 106
Snell, K.D.M. 135, 136, 151
Somerville, A. 136
Sontag, S. 108
Spivak, G.C. 39
Stallybrass, P. 83, 84, 106
Steele, B. 60
Strachey, J. 39, 40, 107

Tennyson, A. 51, 58

Thompson, E.P. 135, 151
Todorov, T. 151
Tolstoy, L. 149
Trollope, A. 119
Tscherning, A. 35
Turner, C.T. 127

Wall, G. 9
Weeks, J. 20, 39
White, A. 83, 84, 106
White, H. 48, 59, 106
Widdowson, P. 111, 113, 114, 126, 147, 148, 152, 153
Widor, K. 33
Williams, R. 29, 40, 46, 59, 106, 108, 130, 131, 134, 138, 150, 151, 153
Wolff, J. 41
Woolf, V. 7, 9, 19, 39, 57, 60
Wordsworth, W. 103
Wotton, G. 30, 40, 46, 59, 105, 108

Young, R. 150

Zohn, H. 40, 41

INDEX OF HARDY'S WORKS

'Barbara of the House of Grebe' 92-108
'Candour in English Fiction' 120
Desperate Remedies 8, 13-41, 117
'The Division' 86, 87
'The Dorsetshire Labourer' 129-50
The Dynasts 23, 43
Far from the Madding Crowd 37
A Group of Noble Dames 93, 105, 107, 108
The Hand of Ethelberta 117
'An Imaginative Woman' 85-92
An Indiscretion in the Life of an Heiress 8, 111-27
'The Ivy-Wife' 87
Jude the Obscure 49, 80, 119, 132, 149
Life's Little Ironies 73

'The Masked Face' 104, 105
The Mayor of Casterbridge 61, 80, 83, 132
'On the Western Circuit' 73-85
'One We Knew' 43, 44
Our Exploits at West Poley 8, 61-72
'The Poor Man and the Lady' 117, 148
The Return of the Native 120, 132, 139-43
'She to Him, II' 33
Tess of the d'Urbervilles 105, 123-26, 131-33, 135, 140, 144, 146, 149, 150
'The Torn Letter' 74
The Trumpet-Major 8, 43-60
Under the Greenwood Tree 37, 117
The Woodlanders 105, 135